POSTCARD HISTORY SERIES

Fort Benton

SURRENDER RIFLE. Fort Benton Civilian Mounted Volunteers fought the Nez Perce at Cow Island and Cow Creek Canyon. Ten days later, Chief Joseph surrendered at the Bear's Paw, handing his rifle to Col. Nelson Miles. Later Colonel Miles presented this historic Winchester 44 Henry Model 1866 carbine to Judge John Tattan of Fort Benton. The rifle, "Golden Boy," now owned by the River and Plains Society, is displayed at the Missouri River Breaks National Monument Interpretive Center. (Photograph by Craig and Liz Larcom; courtesy of River and Plains Society.)

ON THE FRONT COVER: The Yankton, Dakota Territory, levee was lively in the spring of 1874. This real–photo postcard shows three steamboats of the Northwestern Transportation Company, or Coulson Line, waiting to load cargo and depart for Fort Benton. The steamers in the foreground are *Western* and, outboard, *E. H. Durfee*; astern is *Peninah*. (Courtesy of Ken Robison.)

ON THE BACK COVER: Cowboy artist Charles M. Russell, a colorful working cowboy, had many friends in Fort Benton. During September 1904, Russell went by train to Fort Assiniboine to join the 2nd Cavalry for an overland ride to Great Falls. En route, the cavalry camped overnight at Fort Benton. Young Walter B. Dean photographed Russell (right) with two cavalry officers, Capt. F. H. Lawton and an unidentified officer, standing in front of the Joseph Sullivan Saddlery. (Photograph by Walter B. Dean.)

Fort Benton

Enjoy Historic Fort Benton!

Ken Robison

ARCADIA
PUBLISHING

Published by Arcadia Publishing
Charleston SC, Chicago IL, Portsmouth NH, San Francisco CA

Printed in the United States of America

Library of Congress Control Number: 2009920007

For all general information contact Arcadia Publishing at:
Telephone 843-853-2070
Fax 843-853-0044
E-mail sales@arcadiapublishing.com
For customer service and orders:
Toll-Free 1-888-313-2665

Visit us on the Internet at www.arcadiapublishing.com

*To all the recorders of Fort Benton's visual and written history,
past, present, and future; and to all those who appreciate their efforts.*

CONTENTS

ACKNOWLEDGMENTS

My appreciation goes to the following: our dedicated staff of volunteers at the Overholser Historical Research Center—Henry G. Armstrong, Donna Albers, Mary Meissner, Muncie Morger, and Mary Zanto—who join me in preserving and making our historic collections available to the public; our pro bono director, curator, historian, and mentor, John G. Lepley, who dedicates his life to the preservation of Fort Benton's past; our River and Plains Society board members, who guide the museums and share their diverse knowledge and experience; Bob Doerk, our envoy to the Blackfoot; Bruce Druliner; our resident mountain man Burnt Spoon; David Parchen, our artist and fort rebuilder; and Sharalee Smith, our leader on the Old Forts Trail, all of whom bring our history to life with amazing zeal; the hardworking staff Pam Schoonover, Diane Vielleux, Betty Cook, and Ray Scheele, who make the front office hum; James and Cheryl Gagne, the keepers of the jewel in Fort Benton's crown, the Grand Union; Tim Burmeister and Mike Tichenor of the *River Press* for presenting so much history to their readers; the residents of Fort Benton and Chouteau County for caring for their history and sharing their photographs and stories; the Blackfoot Confederacy for caring and sharing our cross-cultural heritage on both sides of the Medicine Line; Doran Degenstein and our many Canadian friends for joining us in preserving our shared regional history; Richard Sims and the Montana Historical Society for constant support and joining so many of our historical events; artist Robert F. Morgan, who visually highlighted our history through his exceptional murals; Fay Todd, whose generosity brought the Bodmer collection and John Mix Stanley's painting of founder Alexander Culbertson to Fort Benton; Dean and Donna Strand for the Milner-Sullivan Ranch collection and for their dedicated support; Tom Mulvaney, Montana's premier postcard collector, who has sent many Fort Benton postcards my way in recent years and kindly shared his personal collection; John Poultney and the staff at Arcadia Publishing for their technical assistance; and, saving the best for last, my wife and world-travelling companion, Michele, for our life of love and shared adventures. Unless otherwise noted, all images are from the author's collection.

INTRODUCTION

Fort Benton on the Upper Missouri is a small town with a big history. It is the birthplace of Montana, the head of navigation on the Missouri River, and important in every era of Montana history. This book highlights the history of Fort Benton through postcard images and interpretive text, presenting the people, places, and events important through the years.

Today it is difficult to appreciate the widespread use of postcards when they were first introduced one century ago. The *Daily Missoulian* in 1911 wrote: "Picture postcards have been like a delightful vice that we first endured, pitied, then embraced. We were inclined to regard the first crude output of them as make-shifts for the lazy and picture cards for the children. Little by little they got in their insidious work—they were such blessed time-savers, they were such inexpensive souvenirs for the folks at home, they were such suggestive mementos of travel! And now we have found that there is no end to their uses, and we buy them by the cartload."

As a timesaving alternative to formal letters, postcards were essentially the e-mail of their day. As you view the postcards in this book, I hope you gain a new appreciation for them.

Fort Benton has been blessed from its beginning with talented historians, artists, and photographers. We owe a great debt to first historian Lt. James G. Bradley, longest resident photographer Daniel Dutro, longest editor of the *River Press* newspaper Joel F. Overholser, teacher and historian John G. Lepley, and artists Karl Bodmer, John Mix Stanley, Gustavus Sohon, James Trott, Brian Morger, and David Parchen for recording, photographing, and drawing the history of the Upper Missouri.

Fort Benton's story begins with the Missouri River and its spectacular natural features along the White Cliffs. The story extends to the American Indian and the buffalo that occupied the land long before the arrival of American explorers and fur traders. Blackfoot Indians long used the natural ford at Fort Benton to cross the Missouri River into Judith and Musselshell hunting grounds. Lewis and Clark made their fateful decision on the course of the Missouri at Decision Point and proceeded on past the Fort Benton river bottom on their journey to the Pacific.

The story spans the fur trade era from the 1830s to the 1860s, when Blackfoot, Gros Ventres, Assiniboin, and Cree traded with St. Louis–based adventurers who moved up the Missouri to establish trading posts. From 1846 to 1847, Alexander Culbertson built Fort Benton as a post for the Upper Missouri Outfit of Pierre Chouteau Jr. and Company, commonly known as the American Fur Company.

In 1859, steamboats arrived a few miles below Fort Benton, delivering trade goods and Native American annuities, and taking furs and buffalo robes downriver to eastern markets. As the head of navigation on the Missouri River, Fort Benton became the hub for the St. Louis–to–Fort Benton steamboat trade from 1859 to 1889, bringing thousands of tons of freight to the frontier.

The year 1860 proved an exciting time at the Fort Benton trading post. Three military groups arrived during July and August that year. First came Maj. George Blake and a military regiment by the steamboats *Chippewa* and *Key West*. Capt. William F. Raynolds arrived on July 14 after coming down the Missouri River from its origin at Three Forks and exploring the Yellowstone Basin. On August 1, Lt. John Mullan arrived at Fort Benton after blazing the Mullan Military Wagon Road from Fort Walla Walla.

With strikes at Gold Creek and Bannack in 1862, Fort Benton became a transportation hub. Fort Benton merchant princes formed trading and freighting empires extending from Fort Benton in every direction, to the mines and camps throughout Montana and northward up the Whoop-Up and Fort Walsh Trails to Canada. Fort Benton supplied military posts at Fort Shaw and Fort Assiniboine. These were wild and woolly days, and the streets of Fort Benton were roamed by the rich and famous, scoundrels and killers, merchants and gamblers, American Indians and soldiers, Irish Fenians and exiled Metis, and, eventually, by women and children.

During the height of the steamboat era, Fort Benton underwent a building boom with many brick buildings replacing original adobe, log, or wood frame buildings. The trading firms powered a vast business empire that, in the words of historian Paul Sharp, made Fort Benton the "Chicago of the Plains." This was a time of made and lost fortunes and of colorful characters.

Railroads brought immense change as Fort Benton shifted to ranching with tens of thousands of cattle and sheep on the open range and large shipments to markets in Chicago. In the early 1900s, the fertile lands of north central Montana opened to dryland farming, with homesteaders arriving by railroad from the east. Fort Benton became the trading center for ranchers and farmers in the heart of what is now "Montana's Golden Triangle" agricultural region.

This history highlights the legends, stories, and people making their mark on each era of the area's history. Sampled are the early Chinese and African Americans who made their mark and then moved on; adventurers like whiskey trader Johnny Healy and fearless lawman X. Beidler; cowboy artist Charlie Russell and his cavalry friends; military leaders and soldiers; and legendary loyal dog Shep. Historic buildings are featured, like the original Block House at Old Fort Benton; the Grand Union Hotel, built at the height of the steamboat era in 1882 and now restored to its elegant grandeur; the grand Chouteau County Court House, built in 1884 and still used today; and the Fort Benton Bridge, which began with a steamboat swing span and continues today as a scenic walking bridge.

Fort Benton became a National Historic Landmark in 1961 and then a Historic District with eight individual buildings on the National Register of Historic Places. Fort Benton is a Preserve America city, on the National Lewis and Clark Historic Trail, and the river entry port for the Upper Missouri, now part of the 149-mile National Wild and Scenic River System and the Upper Missouri Breaks National Historic Landmark. In 2004, Fort Benton became a contributing site on the National Historic Nez Perce Trail in recognition of Fort Benton military and civilian forces at the battles of Cow Island and Cow Creek Canyon.

Fort Benton has four exceptional museums. The Museum of the Northern Great Plains features Montana's State Agricultural Museum, Smithsonian Buffalo, a homestead village, and a community events center. The Museum of the Upper Missouri tells "Twenty Tall Tales of the Upper Missouri," a sampling of Fort Benton's storied past. Old Fort Benton, a combination of the original Block House and reconstructed buildings, forms a fur trading post with a resident role-playing mountain man and displays interpreting Blackfoot culture and fur trading days. The newest is the Upper Missouri Breaks National Monument Interpretive Center, which features Chief Joseph's Surrender Rifle, a replica of the cabin of the steamboat *Far West* with the original bell and telegraph, a full-scale Murphy freighting wagon, and Karl Bodmer's classic scenes from the Upper Missouri. The interpretive center's exterior resembles the White Cliffs of the Missouri.

Today the city of Fort Benton retains much of its "steamboat days" character. The steamboat levee is now a park running the length of the community with many interpretive signs. As you follow the levee trail from the interpretive center downriver to Old Fort Benton, you walk hallowed ground through the pages of history.

One

NATURE'S HIGHWAY
ON THE UPPER MISSOURI

BLACKFOOT YEARS. This 72-by-168-inch oil mural, *Hunt on Arrow Creek, 1700–1831,* by Robert F. Morgan, hangs in the Montana Agricultural Center and features a buffalo hunt with Blackfoot Indians and a buffalo surround. Bison symbolized the West, providing sustenance for American Indians. The end of the buffalo profoundly changed the West. (Photograph by John Godwyn; courtesy of River and Plains Society.)

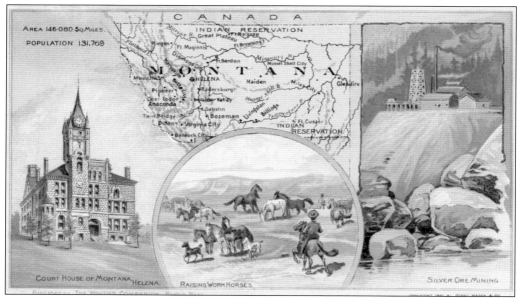

MONTANA STATEHOOD. Issued by *The Youth's Companion*, this card commemorated the new state of Montana in 1889. Its caption notes "Ft. Benton is at the head of the longest river navigation in the world." Fort Benton is the county seat for Choteau County, one of Montana's original nine counties in 1865 and named for fur trader Pierre Chouteau Jr. In 1903, the county name was corrected by the legislature to "Chouteau County." (Courtesy of Tom Mulvaney.)

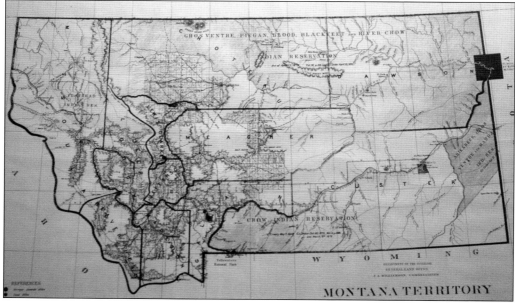

MISSOURI RIVER, 1900. Fort Benton lies in north central Montana at the head of navigation on the Missouri River with major tributaries Yellowstone, Milk, Musselshell, Judith, Marias, and Teton Rivers. Originally, Choteau County extended more than 30,000 square miles from the Rocky Mountains past the Bear's Paw Mountains and from the Judith Basin northward to the Canadian border. Later all or parts of 15 counties were carved from historic Choteau County.

GREETINGS WITH AMERICAN INDIANS. Before Lewis and Clark arrived on the Upper Missouri in 1805, American Indian nations populated the vast land, including Sioux, Assiniboin, Gros Ventres, Crow, Cree, and the Blackfoot Confederacy. The Blackfoot call themselves Nitsitapi, "the One" or "the Real people." Their confederacy comprises four tribes: Siksika or Blackfoot; Kainai or Blood; Pikanii or Northern Peigan; and Pikuni or Southern Piegan, commonly called Blackfeet.

GREETINGS WITH BUFFALO. The Blackfoot Nation extended along the Rockies from present-day Alberta, Canada, southward across the Medicine Line into present-day Montana to the Musselshell River and Three Forks of the Missouri River. Allied with the Blackfoot Nation were the Atsina, or Gros Ventres, and the Sarcee, or Sarsi, who lived proximate to the Blackfoot homeland. Millions of buffalo roamed the lands of the Upper Missouri, providing sustenance for native peoples.

WHITE CLIFFS OF THE MISSOURI. Some 50 miles down the Missouri River from Fort Benton, natural white sandstone formations of stunning beauty line both sides of the river. The White Cliffs of the Missouri continue for a distance of 25 miles with magical castles, sentinels, and tables formed by sills and dikes of Shonkinite granite formations. The granite protrudes from White Eagle sandstone to form famed landmarks. (Courtesy of Overholser Historical Research Center [OHRC].)

MISSOURI RIVER SCENES. This private postcard, printed by the Fort Benton *River Press* about 1900, shows two scenes along the majestic White Cliffs of the Missouri. The upper left presents Le Citadel, today a National Historic Site, named by early French fur trader voyageurs. To the right are the White Cliffs with a stunning collection of churches, chapels, and cathedrals cut from the white sandstone.

EYE OF THE NEEDLE. Across from Eagle Creek, 55 miles below Fort Benton, sandstone alcoves provide spectacular views up and down the river. One sandstone formation known as the Eye of the Needle is shown in this scene. The top of the needle met its demise from youthful vandalism in 1997, several decades before natural erosion might have worn down the top of the needle—a reminder of the fragile nature of sandstone formations. (Courtesy of Karen Bryant.)

WHEN THE LAND BELONGED TO GOD. In 1914, cowboy artist Charles M. Russell captured a classic scene a few miles down the Missouri River from Fort Benton. An endless line of bison cross the river with the Highwood Mountains and Square Butte, called by Capt. Meriwether Lewis "Barn Mountain," in the background. Charlie Russell understood the importance of the bison to Native Americans and lamented their passing from the scene. This painting hangs in the Montana Historical Society in Helena.

BUFFALO LAND. From Texas to the British possessions that became Canada, bison were essential to the Plains Indian culture. The migratory herds roamed the Great Plains of North America. In the words of a Sioux song: "I go to kill the buffalo. The Great Spirit sent the buffalo on hills, in plains and woods. So give me my bow; give me my bow. I go to kill the buffalo."

KING OF AMERICAN BEASTS. In this postcard, photographer Sumner W. Matteson reminded Americans in the early 1900s of the grandeur and importance of the bison in early America. Bison were the basis of American Indian economy for thousands of years. They provided food, clothing, and hides for teepee shelters. Their droppings fueled the campfires, their sinews held garments together, and their bones and horns became tools, utensils, and ornaments.

BISON HUNTERS. The Industrial Revolution fueled demand for buffalo hides to make belts to drive thousands of machines in American and European factories. Over 40 years, thousands of buffalo robes where shipped down river from Fort Benton on steamboats. Bison became an important food for early fur traders, miners, and settlers. In this scene, Henry Bond (far left) and a hunting party shot and hung elk (left) and bison (right). By 1880, bison were disappearing from the plains.

GOVERNMENT HERD. During the winter of 1880, the Canadian herd migrated south, never to return. The last wild herd roamed the Montana Territory between the Missouri and Yellowstone Rivers. The Blackfoot moved into the Judith and Musselshell country for the their last hunt in 1879–1880 before confinement to reservations. Conservationists grew concerned that bison would become extinct. This scene shows a Canadian government–protected bison herd at Banff about 1910.

HORNADAY BISON. Concerned about possible extinction of the bison, in 1886, William T. Hornaday of the Smithsonian came west to collect bison specimens and information for future generations. Six of his specimens were mounted for the Smithsonian's Natural History Museum, where, from 1887 to 1955, these "Hornaday Buffalo" formed the premier display. Today the Hornaday Buffalo are displayed in their natural environment at Fort Benton's Museum of the Northern Great Plains.

BLACKFOOT LODGE. The Blackfoot were nomadic hunter-gatherers living in teepees and subsisting primarily on buffalo and gathered vegetable foods. Blackfoot teepees of buffalo hide were often painted with designs. Blackfoot bison hunters mounted their horses and, with weapons in hand, rode to the prairies for the hunt.

Grand Parade of Blackfoot Indians.

GRAND PARADE. In the spring, bison herds moved out onto grasslands, and the Blackfoot followed. During the summer, they lived in large tribal camps, hunting bison and engaging in ceremonial rituals. In midsummer, the Blackfoot grouped for a major tribal ceremony, the Sun Dance.

Chief Joe Healy and Braves.

WARRIORS. The Sun Dance assembly provided for ceremonial rituals, social intercourse, and warrior societies based on brave acts and deeds. Large bison hunts provided food and offerings for the ceremonies. After the Sun Dance assembly, the Blackfoot once again separated into bands to follow the bison. Chief Joe Healy was a Kainai Indian and the adopted son of Fort Benton trader John J. Healy.

G-54 Chief Mountain

Glacier Studio

5834 CHIEF TWO GUNS WHITE CALF - BLACKFEET INDIAN,
GLACIER NATIONAL PARK, MONTANA.
SEE AMERICA FIRST.

GLACIER NATIONAL PARK. To the Blackfoot, the mountains of Glacier, especially Chief Mountain and the region near Two Medicine, were considered the "Backbone of the World" and were frequented during vision quest rites of passage. In 1895, Chief White Calf, last chief of the Pikuni, authorized the sale of the mountain area, and through the skill of Congressman Charles N. Pray of Fort Benton, Glacier National Park was created in 1910.

CHIEF TWO GUNS WHITE CALF. Two Guns White Calf, youngest son of great Chief White Calf, was born at Fort Benton in 1872. Two Guns White Calf came to symbolize the Blackfeet to passengers visiting Glacier Park on the Great Northern Railroad, greeting them at the East Glacier station. He also traveled widely across the country and became the primary face of the American Indian on the buffalo nickel.

110—INDIAN PONY RACE ON FORT BELKNAP RES'N.

AMERICAN INDIAN HORSES. By 1740, the Blackfoot had horses, and within another decade, horses spread to other northern Plains Indians through extensive native trade networks. American Indians were not dependent on fur traders to acquire horses, and in breeding, handling horses, and riding, northern Plains Indians excelled. Horses fit and extended the hunter-gatherer lifestyle. Horses became essential not only to hunting and migrating, but also to warrior activities in war and peace. Individuals, not the tribe, owned horses, and this produced a class system based on ownership of horses. The vast majority of war parties were to steal horses, not to fight an enemy. These undivided-back postcards show common horse-based activities. (Photographs by Sumner Matteson.)

TRAILING BRUSH FOR THE MEDICINE LODGE

114—ASSINABOINE MEDICINE LODGE.

MORE THAN BLACKFOOT. While much of the Fort Benton trade was with the Blackfoot Nation, important trade was conducted with the Gros Ventres, Cree, and Assiniboin to the north and east. The Assiniboin and their close allies the Cree were intermittently in conflict with the Blackfoot and their Gros Ventres allies. The Assiniboin had long traded with the Canadian-based Hudson's Bay Company and had gained success as traders, horsemen, and respected warriors. The Assiniboin were noted hunters and made greater use of dogs to haul travois loaded with teepee poles, hides, and personal possessions as they followed the buffalo herds during seasonal hunts. The Gros Ventres generally sought good relations with American traders as they followed the buffalo between the Saskatchewan and Missouri Rivers.

"SKY SCRAPERS" OF OTHER DAYS.

Two

FROM PELTS TO ROBES
THE FUR TRADE ERA

DISCOVERY YEARS. This 72-by-204-inch oil mural, *Fortunate Meeting, 1803–1806,* by Robert F. Morgan, hangs in the Montana Agricultural Center. The mural depicts Capt. Meriwether Lewis reuniting his party at the Fort Benton bottom in 1806. The Lewis and Clark Expedition of 1803–1806 opened American fur trading on the Yellowstone and Upper Missouri Rivers. (Photograph by John Godwyn; courtesy of River and Plains Society.)

LEWIS AND CLARK STATE MEMORIAL. In June 1805, the Lewis and Clark Expedition reached Decision Point just below Fort Benton. There the captains made their fateful decision to proceed on to the Pacific Ocean. Before his death in 1926, cowboy artist Charles M. Russell completed drawings for a statue to commemorate the Lewis and Clark Expedition. The 1929 Montana Legislature designated Fort Benton as the site for the memorial but provided no money, so the project stalled. Montana's premier sculptor, Bob Scriver, and Fort Benton leaders revived the effort in 1973, and the Montana State Memorial was completed as a privately funded National Bicentennial Project. Dedicated on June 13, 1976, the statue is in an honored location on the Fort Benton steamboat levee. Scriver's heroic 21-foot-tall statue, mounted on local Square Butte Quarry granite, depicts Capt. William Clark with a rifle, Capt. Meriwether Lewis with a telescope, and Shoshone woman Sacagawea with her son Pomp.

FORT BENTON, 1853. By 1830, Fort Union, at the confluence of the Yellowstone, was established, and the American fur trade era had begun. This image of the trading post at Fort Benton is a lithographic print published in volume XII, part one of the *Reports of Explorations and Surveys to Ascertain the Most Practicable and Economic Route for a Railroad from the Mississippi River to the Pacific Ocean.* The print was derived from a watercolor by John Mix Stanley during his 1853 visit to Fort Benton with Gov. Isaac I. Stevens and the 1853–1855 Northern Railroad Survey Expedition. These volumes constitute the most important contemporary source of knowledge on geography and history of the Upper Missouri. While Stanley had photographic equipment with him, no photographs have been found, and this is the first known visual image of Fort Benton.

FIRST PHOTOGRAPH, 1860. The year 1860 proved an exciting time in early Fort Benton history with the arrival of the first steamboats at the levee and three important military expeditions. First Lt. John Mullan led a road-building expedition into Fort Benton on August 1st after blazing a military wagon road from Fort Walla Walla in the Washington Territory. Maj. George Blake of the 1st Dragoons arrived at Fort Benton with a 300-man expedition on July 2, 1860, by the steamboats

Chippewa and *Key West* to join Lieutenant Mullan. Capt. William F. Raynolds and his party came down the Missouri past the Great Falls of the Missouri after exploring the Yellowstone River basin, arriving at Fort Benton on the evening of July 14th. James Dempsey Hutton accompanied Captain Raynolds and took the first known image of Fort Benton looking westward from across the Missouri River. (Courtesy of OHRC.)

RUINS OF OLD FORT BENTON

GREETINGS FROM MONTANA

CHRISTMAS, 1850. In 1846, Maj. Alexander Culbertson began a new trading post several miles below Fort Lewis. Later adobe brick buildings replaced the logs, with the first building completed in December 1850 and dedicated by a big dance on Christmas night. Late that night, Culbertson named the post for Sen. Thomas H. Benton of Missouri. This proposal met with instant acclaim, and the dance resumed at Fort Benton. (Courtesy of Tom Mulvaney.)

ALEXANDER CULBERTSON. Alexander Culbertson and his Kainai Indian wife Natoyist-Siksina' or Natawista built a cross-cultural society at Fort Benton. As head factor, interpreter, and U.S. special agent, Culbertson built close relations with the Blackfoot Nation. In 1856, John Mix Stanley painted this oil portrait of Alexander Culbertson, the greatest of the Upper Missouri fur traders and founder of Fort Benton. Stanley's painting hangs today in the Museum of the Northern Great Plains.

WARPING THE BOAT. The fur trade came to the Upper Missouri on the heels of the Lewis and Clark Expedition. Boats that carried trade goods upriver and brought furs down were man-powered wooden craft. Dugouts, mackinaws, and keelboats had to be laboriously warped or cordelled, rowed, or poled by hardworking men. The journey from St. Louis began early in the spring and continued slowly up 2,360 miles to the Upper Missouri. (Art by John Innes.)

FUR TRADE WORKHORSE. Before steamboats, keelboats were the largest and most widely used craft. About 70 feet in length and 18 feet on the beam, they carried 25 to 30 tons of cargo and arrived at Fort Benton at the American Fur Company trading post or at Robert Campbell's opposition post, Fort Campbell. This exact replica of the keelboat *Mandan* was built by MGM for use in the movie *The Big Sky*. Since 1965, the keelboat *Mandan* has been high and dry on the Fort Benton levee.

BLACKFOOT FUR TRADE. The first post in Blackfoot country was Fort Piegan in 1831, followed by Fort MacKenzie in 1832, Fort Lewis in 1845, and opposition forts. This postcard depicts reconstructed Old Fort Benton with its original Block House, the last vestige of the fur trade and Montana's oldest standing structure. Other views show the Old Fort Benton Museum with original artifacts and interpretation of Blackfoot culture and the fur trade. (Photographs by Sharalee Smith.)

OLD FORT BENTON.   BUILT IN 1846.   *Montana*

OLD FORT BENTON. This private postcard shows Old Fort Benton in the 1870s. The early log buildings had been replaced during the 1850s by adobe brick. Bourgeois Alexander Culbertson, agent-in-charge at the post, and his Blackfoot wife, Natawista, lived in the quarters on the second floor of the Bourgeois House. Other buildings included the Trade Store/Warehouse, Engages' Quarters, Blacksmith/Carpenter Shop, Kitchen, Barn, and two Block Houses at the northeast and southwest corners. (Courtesy of Tom Mulvaney.)

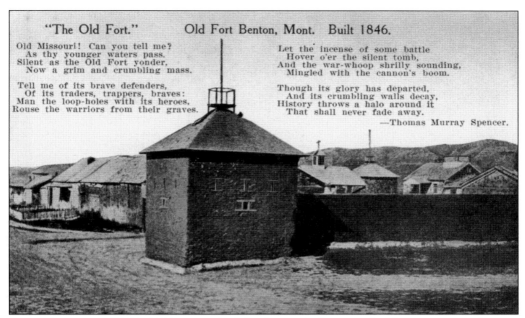

"The Old Fort."　　Old Fort Benton, Mont.　Built 1846.

Old Missouri! Can you tell me?
　As thy younger waters pass.
Silent as the Old Fort yonder,
　Now a grim and crumbling mass.

Tell me of its brave defenders,
　Of its traders, trappers, braves:
Man the loop-holes with its heroes,
Rouse the warriors from their graves.

Let the incense of some battle
　Hover o'er the silent tomb,
And the war-whoop shrilly sounding,
　Mingled with the cannon's boom.

Though its glory has departed,
　And its crumbling walls decay,
History throws a halo around it
　That shall never fade away.
　　　　　　　—Thomas Murray Spencer.

"THE OLD FORT." This 1913 postcard of the fort carried a poem by Thomas Murray Spencer paying tribute to the Missouri River, Old Fort Benton, and its trailblazers. "Tell me of its brave defenders. / Of its traders, trappers, braves. . . . / Though its glory has departed, / and its crumbling walls decay, / History throws a halo around it / That shall never fade away." These were prophetic words written a century ago.

FUR FORT, 1880s. This undivided-back postcard shows the deterioration of Old Fort Benton during the 1880s as the adobe walls began to crumble. This scene looks north with the long Trade Store/Warehouse and surviving Block House on the right. The Engages' Quarters stand on the left with the crumbling Bourgeois Quarters and second Block House. (Photograph by Dan Dutro; courtesy of Tom Mulvaney.)

Fur Trade Symposium 2003

Fort Benton, Montana
September 18, 19, 20, 2003

©

FUR TRADE SYMPOSIUM. Thomas Murray Spencer would have been proud when, a century later, from September 18 to 20, 2003, Fort Benton hosted the triennial National Fur Trade Symposium. This postcard invited international attendees to the event. The scene, painted by artist David Parchen, shows the American Fur Company trading post at Fort Benton as it appeared in 1855, with a keelboat in the foreground.

The Ruins of Old Fort Benton

K 712

OLD FORT BENTON, LATE 1890S. The rapid deterioration of the fort's adobe buildings is apparent in this photograph from the late 1890s. From left to right in the scene looking east are the northeast Block House, the east wall of the Engages' Quarters with an unidentified rider, the west wall of the Engages' Quarters, and the Fort Benton Bridge across the Missouri River. (Photograph by Morris and Kirby, Chinook, Montana.)

OLD FORT BENTON, EARLY 1900s. Further deterioration of the west wall of the Engages' Quarters is apparent in this photograph, taken about 1900, looking northeast. The Block House entrance is shown in this view. In the early 1900s, Thomas C. Power and Brother, with help from the Daughters of the American Revolution, led an effort to save the Block House, beginning with wood wainscot framing to shore up the walls.

Ruins of For   , Montana, 1846—1907.

OLD FORT BENTON, 1907. By 1907, the exterior of the Block House was encased in concrete to protect the adobe bricks from further deterioration. Visible on the far left of this scene is part of the Isaac G. Baker warehouse. Note the absence of trees in the fort area at this time. (Courtesy of Tom Mulvaney.)

OLD FORT BENTON, 1920s. Before 1910, the first trees were planted in the fort area, and by the early 1920s, their growth was clearly visible. The walls of the Block House were encased in concrete, and the historic building was preserved. The walls of the Engages' Quarters continued to deteriorate. The cannon on the left was an 1864 Civil War cannon probably brought to Fort Benton by the army in 1869.

OLD FORT PARK, 1930s. By the 1930s, the character of Old Fort Benton was changing. The trees now provided shade, and Old Fort Park became a popular picnicking site. Signage was added commemorating the fort and the founding of Fort Benton. The sign reads "Fort Benton Mont. Est. 1846 By Alexander Culbertson of the American Fur Co. City Surveyed by Col. De'Lacey in 1859 [*sic*]. Chouteau County Estab. Feb. 2, 1865 and Named in Honor of Pierre Chouteau, President of American Fur Co., Original Stockade Quadrangle 300 Feet Square, Flanked on Each Diagonal Corner." Walter W. De Lacy, a civil engineer and surveyor in the early Montana Territory, surveyed the town of Fort Benton in 1865.

OLD FORT, 1950s. The original fort was built in a quadrangle over 150 feet square exclusive of the 20-foot square two-story bastion Block Houses. Portholes in bastion walls afforded both cannon and riflemen command of a shooting range on every side. The roof and exterior of the surviving Block House by this time were well preserved. By the 1950s, sentiment in the community was building to preserve Fort Benton history.

THE RIVER AND THE LEVEE. The Fort Benton waterfront and levee had come a long way since the fur trade, when there were no trees and the ground was barren. In this view, Signal Point bluff dominates the background as the river flows by. During steamboat days, an observer on Signal Point would alert the town of steamboat arrivals. The Civil War cannon is in a place of honor on the levee.

MULLAN ROAD. The Mullan Military Wagon Road was the first wagon road to cross the Rocky Mountains from the head of navigation on the Missouri River to the head of navigation on the Columbia. Leaving Fort Walla Walla, Washington Territory, in June 1859, First Lt. John Mullan led an expedition that carved a 624-mile wagon road through the mountains of Idaho into Montana, arriving at Fort Benton on August 1, 1860. Over the years, segments of the historic road became Montana's Benton Road from Fort Benton to Helena; the Northern Pacific Railroad from Helena over Mullan Pass to Missoula; and Interstate Highway 90 from western Montana to Spokane, Washington. The postcard above shows an obelisk monument to Capt. John Mullan at the entrance to Old Fort Park, while the view below shows a Mullan Road sign in the park.

MULLAN MONUMENT, AND RUINS OF OLD FORT BENTON MONT.

CAPT. JOHN MULLAN, FORT BENTON, MONT.

JOHN MULLAN MONUMENT. Much of the Mullan Road followed old American Indian trails. During the expedition and two years of further improvements, Lieutenant Mullan and his military and civilian workforce hacked the 25-foot-wide road through 125 miles of timber, dug 30 miles of excavation, and built hundreds of bridges. The Mullan Road was designated a historic site by the National Resister of Historic Places in 1975. The American Society of Civil Engineers designated it a Historic Civil Engineering Landmark in 1977. Many markers and signs commemorate the Mullan Road. These views show the marble obelisk with bas relief figure of Capt. John Mullan, which was dedicated in an impressive ceremony in Old Fort Park by Gov. Samuel V. Stewart at the Chouteau County Fair on September 20, 1917. In recent years, the Mullan Monument has been relocated to the Fort Benton levee.

Three

GOING TO
THE MOUNTAINS
STEAMBOATS AND
OVERLAND FREIGHTING

HO! FOR THE GOLD FIELDS, 1862–1874. This 72-by-132-inch oil mural by Robert F. Morgan hangs in the Montana Agricultural Center, symbolizing the wild and woolly years that followed the fur trade era. Fueled by gold strikes in the southwestern Montana Territory, steamboats brought thousands up the Missouri River to seek their fortunes in the placer gold camps. (Photograph by John Godwyn; courtesy of River and Plains Society.)

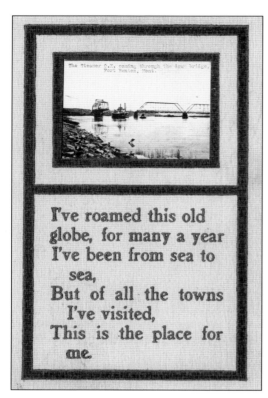

I've roamed this old
globe, for many a year
I've been from sea to
 sea,
But of all the towns
 I've visited,
This is the place for
 me.

HEAD OF NAVIGATION. Steamboating and overland freighting are the themes of these two Fort Benton greeting cards from around 1910. The card at left symbolizes the steamboat era and shows the small steamer *O.K.* in 1907 coming through the open swing span on the Fort Benton Bridge. The card below shows immense Murphy wagons hauling steamboat freight from Fort Benton along the Benton Road to Helena and other frontier settlements in the days of the Montana Territory. The greetings boast generically about the town and climate, and "from sea to sea . . . this is the place for me." (Both, courtesy of Tom Mulvaney.)

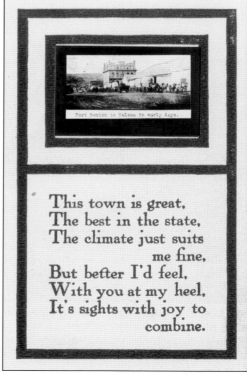

This town is great,
The best in the state,
The climate just suits
  me fine,
But better I'd feel,
With you at my heel,
It's sights with joy to
  combine.

FORT BENTON LEVEE. From 1860 to 1890, Fort Benton's 1.5-mile levee was filled with steamboats, massive piles of freight, and hundreds of freight wagons, providing Montana and southern Canada with 150,000 tons of commerce worth $300 million. Downriver went over a million buffalo robes, valuable furs, more than 100 tons of gold, hundreds of cattle, and millions of pounds of wool. Thousands of men made their livelihood steamboating, freighting, and retailing this vast trade.

ST. LOUIS STEAMBOAT LEVEE. From St. Louis, steamboats traveled more than 2,300 miles to reach the Fort Benton levee. The vast levee at St. Louis was crowded with hundreds of steamboats heading north and south on the Mississippi River, east on the Ohio River, and west up the Missouri River. During the 1860s, St. Louis monopolized the Montana trade until railroads reached Sioux City, then Yankton, and finally Bismarck. (Photograph by R. Goebel.)

DeSMET AT FORT BENTON LEVEE. The steamboat *DeSmet*, built in 1872, was named for early missionary Fr. Jean Pierre DeSmet, a frequent traveler to the Upper Missouri. Capt. Joseph LaBarge brought the *DeSmet* to Fort Benton in 1873 with 31 passengers and 230 tons freight, arriving on June 29th, only to find the boat impounded for selling whiskey to Native Americans. Departure was delayed for more than two weeks while LaBarge traveled to Helena to gain the release of his steamboat.

R. GOEBEL PHOTO   OLDEN TIMES ON THE MISSOURI RIVER, 1880   NO. 19
St. Charles, Mo..

LOADING GENERAL MEADE. The *General Meade* made many trips to Fort Benton in the late 1870s. This scene has the steamboat being loaded at St. Charles, Missouri, by African Americans for a trip to the mountains. Many steamboats had black or immigrant crews. Several early black residents of Fort Benton worked their way up the river on steamboats, including sisters Maria and Mary Adams, who had worked for Gen. George and Elizabeth Custer until his death. (Photograph by R. Goebel.)

STEAMBOAT PASSENGER PASS. Steamboat passengers carried postcard–sized passes printed with details about scheduled departures and agents. This rare card for the St. Louis–based Montana and Idaho Transportation Line was used for travel on the steamboat *Agnes* departing St. Louis on April 27, 1867, for "Ft. Benton, Helena, Virginia City And all Points in the Mining Districts." The line, owned by young John G. Copelin and his father-in-law, John J. Roe, dominated the mountain trade from 1864 to 1868. Their steamboat operations were uniquely integrated with overland freighting and retail merchandising. The back of each passenger pass showed distances from St. Louis to Fort Benton with major waypoints and distances indicated. Note the distance to Fort Benton in 1867 was 2,965 miles. The *Agnes* arrived at Fort Benton on July 5th with 35 passengers and 160 tons of freight after an arduous 68–day trip.

1867 HO! FOR THE 1867
GOLD MINES!
THE MONTANA AND IDAHO
Transportation Line
WILL GIVE
THROUGH BILLS LADING
FOR
FT. BENTON, HELENA, VIRGINIA CITY
And all Points in the
MINING DISTRICTS

The Splendid and Light Draught Steamers of this Line

WILL LEAVE ST. LOUIS AS FOLLOWS,

AMELIA POE,	G. A. THOMPSON,
Saturday, March 16.	Tuesday, March 26.
YORKTOWN,	DEER LODGE,
Saturday, March 23.	Wednesday, April 3.
NYMPH, NO. 2	BERTHA,
Sunday, March 24.	Friday, April 5.

☞ Other Boats will be started as may be Required.

All Steamers of this Line Class A No. 1.

For Freght or Passage apply to
JOHN G. COPELIN, Agent,
South-East Corner Main and Olive streets.

JOS. McENTIRE, Agent,
No. 312 (new No.) Commercial street, bet. Olive & Locust.

DISTANCES
FROM
ST. LOUIS TO FORT BENTON.

From St. Louis to—

Jefferson City	174
Lexington	374
Kansas City	456
Leavenworth	495
St. Joseph	565
Omaha	807
Sioux City	1010
Yancton	1181
Bonhomme Island	1211
Fort Randall	1285
Fort Thompson (Crow Creek)	1441
Fort Sully	1520
Old Fort Pierre	1525
Big Cheyenne	1585
Little Cheyenne River	1640
Moreau	1670
Fort Rice	1810
Square Bute	1895
Fort Berthold	1985
Little Missouri	2015
Mouth Yellowstone	2235
Fort Union (Ft. Buford)	2240
Milk River	2482
Fort Copelin	2497
Fort Galpin	2502
Muscle Shell River	2678
Dry Point	2698
Cow Island	2793
Camp Cook, Judith river	2848
Drowned Man's Rapids	2851
Maras River	2938
Fort Benton	2965

From Fort Benton to—

Helena	150
Prickly Pear	170
Last Chance	171
Deer Lodge City	180
Deer Lodge Diggings	210
Virginia City	270
Bannock City	300
Gallatin	350
Bosman	351

DISTANCES

BETWEEN

SAINT LOUIS AND FORT BENTON.

Jefferson City		174	Grand River..*700*..	31..	1721	
Boonville	58..	232	Beaver River..*1780*..	85..	1806	
Glasgow	32..	264	Canon Ball River *1800*..	30..	1836	
Brunswick	35..	299	Fort Rice..*1810*..	10..	1846	
Lexington	75..	374	Hart River..*1860*..	50..	1896	
Kansas City	82..	456	Old Fort Clarke *1925*..	65..	1961	
Leavenworth City	39..	495	Fort Berthold..*1985*..	59..	2020	
Atchison	37..	532	Little Missouri..*2015*..	30..	2050	
St. Joseph	33..	565	White Earth River *2090*..	85..	2135	
Nebraska City	175..	740	Mouth Yellowstone *2235*..135..		2270	
Council Bluffs	53..	793	Fort Union..*2240*..	5..	2275	
Omaha	14..	807	Milk River..*2482*..350..		2625	
Florence	15..	822	Round Bute..*2593*..135..		2760	
Little Sioux River	72..	894	Dophan's Rapids *2927*.152..		2912	
Sioux City	116..	1010	Mouth Maria..*2935*..218..		3130	
Vermillion River	140..	1150	Fort Benton..*2965*..	45..	3175	
James River	47..	1197	Judith		2848	
Yancton	4..	1201				
Bonhomme Island	16..	1217	**From FORT BENTON to**			
Mouth Niobrarah	22..	1239	Silver City	150		
Yancton Agency	32..	1271	Prickley Pear	170		
Fort Randall	14..	1285	Last Chance	171		
White River..*1405*..106..		1391	Deer Lodge City	180		
Crow Creek or Ush- *1441*			Deer Lodge Diggins	210		
ers' Landing	94..	1485	Virginia City	270		
Fort Sully..*1520*..	45..	1530	Bannock City	300		
Fort Pierre..*1525*..	5..	1535	Gallatin	350		
Big Cheyenne..*1545*..55..		1590	Bosman	351		
Mouth Moreau..*1670*..100..		1690				

MILITARY PASSENGER PASS. Lt. Col. George L. Andrews of the 13th Infantry Regiment used this exceptional pre–postcard–era card when the regiment departed Omaha on May 23, 1866, on the steamboat *Henry S. Turner* to go to Fort Sully, Dakota Territory. Note the postmark "Missouri River May 23 1866 *Henry S. Turner*" on the card. In June, Lieutenant Colonel Andrews took the card with him when he continued up the Missouri River on the steamer *Deer Lodge* on an assignment to select a location at the mouth of the Judith River for the first military post in the northern Montana Territory. Lieutenant Colonel Andrews marked corrected mileage as the *Deer Lodge* made its way up the river, and he wrote "Judith 2848 miles." *Deer Lodge* arrived at the mouth of the Judith on July 11, leaving Lieutenant Colonel Andrews and elements of the 13th Infantry together with 147 tons of construction material to build Camp Cooke.

ROSE BUD UNDERWAY. Built in 1877 for the mountain trade, the steamboat *Rose Bud* had a narrow beam, spoonbill bow, and shallow draft, and it handled Upper Missouri hazards well through most water conditions. In this view, the *Rose Bud* is underway at Drowned Man's Rapids above the Judith River. The *Rose Bud*'s trips to Fort Benton in 1889 made her one of the last two commercial steamboats to arrive at the head of navigation.

THE FAMED *FAR WEST*. This Coulson Line steamboat gained fame with her captain, Grant Marsh, making 23 trips to the Upper Missouri, often winning the horns as the fastest boat on the river. During the Terry/Custer Expedition of June 1876, the *Far West* supported operations on the Yellowstone River, and after Custer's defeat, Captain Marsh brought the *Far West*, with 138 wounded men, 710 miles downriver to safety in just 54 hours, a legendary feat.

THE MEAGHER MYSTERY. Colorful Irish revolutionary hero Thomas Francis Meagher escaped British custody to the United States, heroically led the Irish Brigade during the Civil War, and came west as secretary to the governor of the Montana Territory. As acting governor, he organized the Montana Militia to face the Native American threat. At midday on July 1, 1867, General Meagher rode into Fort Benton with an escort of six men to take a steamboat down to Camp Cooke to receive arms shipments. After spending the afternoon at the Isaac G. Baker store and eating supper at Baker's house, Meagher boarded the steamboat *G.A. Thomson* for the night. He was never seen again, and his body was never found. Did he die from vigilante justice? Fall from a weakened railing? Jump in frustration over failed finances? That is the great mystery of General Meagher's death in Fort Benton.

Meagher Monument Helena, Mont.

THOS. MEAGHER

THOMAS FRANCIS MEAGHER.

Irish patriot and American soldier and statesman. Condemned to death in the Irish rebellion of 1848. Sentence changed to transportation for life. Escaped from Australia and came to United States. Raised and organized Irish Brigade and personally commanded it in the battles of Fair Oaks, Mechanicsville, Gaines' Mill, White Oaks Swamp, Malvern Hill, Fredericksburg, Antietam and Chancellorsville. Appointed Major General, 1864. Acting governor of Montana from September 1865, to July 1, 1867, when he was drowned in Missouri river at Fort Benton.

MEAGHER'S SPEECH WHEN CONDEMNED TO DEATH.

"I am not here to crave with faltering lip the life I have consecrated to the independance of my country. . . . I offer to my country, as some proof of the sincerity with which I have thought and spoken and struggled for her, the life of a young heart. . . . The history of Ireland explains my crime and justifies it. . . . Even here where the shadows of death surround me, and from which I see my grave opening for me in no consecrated soil, the hope which beckoned me forth on that perilous sea whereon I have been wrecked, animates, consoles, enraptures me. No I do not despair of my poor old country, her peace, her liberty, her glory."

COULSON STEAMBOAT OFFICE. The Missouri River Transportation Company, or Coulson Line, operated steamboats on the Upper Missouri. From 1879 to 1883, the Coulson Line built and operated the three largest steamboats ever to reach the upper river: *Montana*, *Dacotah*, and *Wyoming*. These sister boats were huge 262-foot stern wheelers weighing more than 900 tons and capable of handling over 600 tons of freight. The image above shows the Coulson Steamboat Office on the upper levee in Fort Benton, built in 1881 by agent Col. George Clendenin. Long after the end of the steamboat years, this building served colorfully as a dance hall, law offices, a lodge hall, a brothel, and an apartment. The photograph below shows the Coulson Office undergoing demolition in 2001. Tragically, this removed the final direct vestige of steamboat operations at Fort Benton. (Photographs by Ken Robison.)

STEAMBOAT *O.K.* This undivided-back postcard from 1906 shows the small 60-ton steamboat *O.K.* tied up along shore on the Missouri River. Written on the postcard is "All aboard for down the Missouri. Taking on coal at a point along the banks. Trip made Sept. 9, 1906. Coal mines along the bluffs at left. L.P.A."

_O.K._ AT SWING SPAN. The *O.K.* arrived at Fort Benton on August 24, 1907, brought up river by Capt. George Stevens, the new owner of the Grand Union Hotel. The next day, the drawbridge swung open to let the boat upstream to anchor at the levee by the hotel. On her way through the swing span, the *O.K.* hit one of the bridge piers, damaging the pier and removing part of the boat's cabin.

337 A. Steamboat " O. K.," at head of Navigation, Fort Benton, Montana 1907.
Geo. W. Crane, Publisher.

O.K. AT FORT BENTON LEVEE, 1907. The *O.K.*, at 115 feet in length, was about half of the full steamboat size. She made several sightseeing excursions up the river above Fort Benton, several passenger trips, and one freight run downriver in her short life at the head of navigation. This view shows the *O.K.* above the Fort Benton Bridge, moored by the Grand Union Hotel.

STEAMBOAT O.K. IN 1908

STEAMBOAT *O.K.*, 1908. Unlike the port of Bismarck, Fort Benton had no boat ways, so for the winter of 1907–1908, Captain Stevens pulled the *O.K.* up on the riverbank to protect her from winter ice. She was left high and dry on the bank when the flood of June 1908 occurred, and reconstruction of the bridge without a swing span imprisoned her there. (Courtesy of OHRC.)

BURNED OUT O.K. The steamer *O.K.* burned on June 30, 1908, some say from arson for insurance money. This postcard shows the burned hull of the *O.K.* with the note "This is a steamboat at Ft Benton was partly burned last summer was a passenger boat called the *O.K.* Billie Baker." Later the tiny 71-foot stern wheeler *Baby Rose* operated commercially from Fort Benton in 1909 before being crushed by winter ice.

STEAMBOAT *MANDAN*. The steamboat *Mandan*, a snag boat used to clear Missouri River hazards to navigation, became the last steamboat to ascend the river to Fort Benton. Its arrival on June 20, 1921, afforded residents of Fort Benton their last look at a steamboat at their levee and marked the end of an era. (Courtesy of OHRC.)

BENTON BELLE. After the restoration and reopening of the historic 1882 Grand Union Hotel on the Fort Benton levee in 1999, the small passenger boat *Benton Belle* was trucked to Fort Benton and moored by the hotel levee to provide passenger excursions up the Missouri River. By then, motorized traffic had a "no-wake" speed restriction downriver from Fort Benton.

BENTON BELLE UNDERWAY. For several years, the *Benton Belle* added a missing element to the Fort Benton waterfront. Unfortunately, the boat was not designed for shallow-draft operations, and water conditions provided problems. After several years of operations, the *Benton Belle* was lost to Fort Benton. Mackinaws, rafts, canoes, and other non-motorized boats still operate during boating season, but the steamboats are gone forever.

THE JERKLINE. Before railroads, the arrival of a steamboat with hundreds of tons of freight destined for frontier mining camps and settlements meant a monumental challenge for overland freighting. Cowboy artist Charles M. Russell painted *The Wagon Boss* and *The Jerkline* depicting these colorful freighters in action. The wagon master cracks his bullwhip as his mules strain to pull loaded wagons up the trail. What a sight!

OX TEAM AT FORT BENTON. In the 1860s, the Fort Benton levee was piled with hundreds of tons of freight off-loaded from arriving steamboats. Hundreds of wagons and men and thousands of oxen, mules, and horses were loading, unloading, or moving along the trails leading in every direction from Fort Benton. This ox train is loaded and waiting to move out by the Murphy Neel and Company store.

50

JERKLINE MULE TRAIN. Some 500 wagons gathered at Fort Benton each year as navigation opened on the river. Wagon trains involved up to 250 wagons and 300 men. From four to eight yoke of oxen drew each wagon, and such a train made a stunning show. This mule train is loaded by the store of Thomas C. Power and Brother. The legendary freighting outfit Diamond R Overland's line grew to immense proportions.

OVERLAND FREIGHTING. At the peak of steamboat traffic in 1881, seventeen thousand tons of freight, in the estimation of historian Joel F. Overholser, required a minimum of 1,700 three-wagon loads, more than 1,000 wagons at five trips in a season, over 400 men, and 5,000 animals. Trails led in every direction: Cow Island Trail, Northern Overland Road, Mullan Road, Benton Road to Helena, Virginia City Road, and many others.

"MUD WAGON" STAGE. In the 1860s, passengers arrived by steamboat anxious to move on from Fort Benton's Spartan conditions to final destinations. These adventurers moved on by horse, foot, wagon, or stage. The stagecoaches were "mud wagons" like that shown in this view, stripped-down Concord coaches for the Montana trade. In good weather, the stage along the Benton Road to Helena took two days and two nights for a $25 fare.

BENTON STAGE, 1894. The first stage on a reorganized line from Fort Benton to Lewistown, Montana, left Fort Benton on July 4, 1894, for the 13-hour trip. The first stage carried the Fort Benton Brass Band to play at each stop along the way. Oscar Johnston, manager of the stage line, is shown driving the second passenger coach with the Grand Union Hotel in the background. (Photograph by Dan Dutro; courtesy of OHRC.)

WHOOP-UP TRAIL. In 1869, John Healy and Al Hamilton took a wagon north from Fort Benton along the Whoop-Up Trail to establish a trading post across the Medicine Line on the Belly River. They built Fort Whoop-Up and realized a profit of $40,000 the first season. For five years, heavy freight wagons streamed north up the trail. This marker in Fort Benton commemorates the wild and woolly years at Whoop-Up.

FORT BENTON-FORT MACLEOD TRAIL MARKER at Fort Benton

INSCRIPTION ON MARKER

The Fort Benton to Fort Mac-Leod or "Whoop-Up" trail into Canada was the main artery of commerce in the 1869-1883 era. Twenty yoke of oxen was a team and each team hauled three of the heavy freight wagons loaded with trade goods, calico and whiskey. They returned loaded with hides for the St. Louis market. Until the closing of the river trade this road was the source of supply for the Royal Canadian Mounted Police, the Boundary Survey and the Canadian Pacific Railway. The resourceful, fearless plainsmen and bull-whackers relaxed at the end of their hazardous journey, opened their cargo, not the calico, and "whooped it up." Thus the name "Fort Whoop-Up" and the famous "Whoop-Up Trail."

Placing of this marker in Old Fort Park was sponsored by Fort Benton M. I. A. history group

WHOOP UP TRAIL MARKER. Trade goods, rifles, food, and whiskey barrels headed north from Fort Benton. At the end of the long journey up the Whoop-Up Trail, bullwhackers relaxed, tapped their barrels, and "whooped it up." Wagons returned loaded with hides for eastern markets. Until the Canadian Pacific Railroad arrived in 1883, Fort Benton supplied robe traders, North West Mounted Police, and early settlers of southern Canada. (Courtesy of OHRC.)

FORT MACLEOD. The wild years at Fort Whoop-Up and other "whiskey forts" led to the arrival of the North West Mounted Police in 1874 to bring law and order to southwestern Canada. Led by Col. James F. Macleod, the mounted police established Forts Macleod and Walsh. Fort Benton–based whiskey traders saw that their days were numbered after the arrest of trader John D. Weatherwax by the mounties and withdrew south of the border.

NORTH WEST MOUNTED POLICE. Ironically, Fort Benton became a base of support for the North West Mounted Police, providing their transportation network and logistical supplies. Merchants Isaac G. Baker and Thomas C. Power contracted with the Canadian government to bring men and material by steamboats to Fort Benton and by wagons overland up the Whoop-Up or Fort Walsh Trails. Until the arrival of the Canadian Pacific in 1883, all men and support came via Fort Benton.

Four

GOLDEN YEARS
BUILDING THE TOWN

BAKER STREET EMPIRE, 1875–1887. This 84-by-240-inch oil mural by Robert F. Morgan hangs in the Montana Agricultural Center. The mural shows a bustling street in Fort Benton in the early 1880s, featuring bullwhackers, cowboys, ox teams, townspeople, and two boys and their dog. (Photograph by John Godwyn; courtesy of River and Plains Society.)

FORT BENTON PANORAMA, 1907. This postcard panoramic view of Fort Benton looking west was taken in 1907. On the right is the Fort Benton Bridge with its west swing span allowing steamboats to pass up river. The small steamboat *O.K.* is moored along the levee near the Grand Union Hotel just upriver from the bridge. The two-story Coulson Line Office is visible near the river, right of center, while the Chouteau County Court House is behind the Coulson building.

This photograph was taken from the Look Out bluffs east and just across the river. This undivided-back postcard notes that Fort Benton is "The oldest established town in Montana, built 1846. The head of navigation on the Missouri." The sender added "What do you think of this town?" (Photograph by Charles E. Morris, Chinook, Montana.)

GRAND VIEW, 1912–1913. During the summers of 1912 and 1913, photographer Evelyn J. Cameron visited the Square Butte Ranch southeast of Fort Benton for bird-watching. Cameron took this excellent-quality view from the bluffs east of town. In the foreground is the Edward Smith home. The three-story Grand Union Hotel is centered in the photograph. The Fort Benton Bridge is on the right. (Courtesy of Tom Mulvaney.)

FORT BENTON DOWN RIVER. This view, taken around 1920, looks north down the Missouri River toward the Fort Benton Bridge and the bend in the river by Signal Point. In the background are two large grain elevators along the Great Northern Railroad line. The well-developed Chouteau County fairgrounds and racetrack are visible in the foreground. The scene looks over Roosevelt Island, named for early Wells Fargo agent Ferdinand C. Roosevelt.

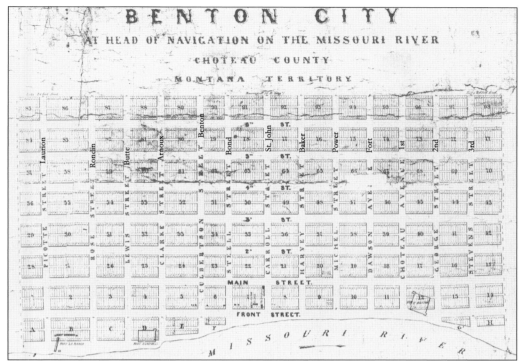

FORT BENTON PLAT. Civil engineer Walter W. De Lacy surveyed the town of Fort Benton, developing the first plat in 1865. Original names shown on this plat were changed in 1884 to the names shown to the right of each original name. Merchants Thomas C. Power and Isaac G. Baker replaced older names like Lewis and Clark. More recently, the names of all east-west streets were changed to numbers.

FORT BENTON RIVER PARK. By 1890, the Fort Benton levee was no longer piled with goods awaiting overland freighting. The town developed the riverfront with trees and parks. The Fort Benton City Park was formed between the Grand Union Hotel and the Fire Engine House. By the 1900s, trees were well developed, lights were in place, and a gazebo was located in the center of the park. (Courtesy of OHRC.)

STOCKMEN'S BANK BLOCK, 1920. By 1920, this block showed change, with a three-story brick building just south (left) of Stockmen's National Bank. The new building housed, from right to left, Walter J. Minar's Drug Store, Emil Bratz's Billiard Hall, and the Louther Funeral Home.

STOCKMEN'S BANK BLOCK, 1920. By 1920, this block showed change, with a three-story brick building just south (left) of Stockmen's National Bank. The new building housed, from right to left Walter J. Minar's Drug Store; Emil Bratz's Billiard Hall; and the Louther Funeral Home.

BANK BLOCK, 1929. This scene looks north, not west as marked on the postcard, and on Front Street, not Main Street, showing the Grand Union Hotel on the right. On the left is a good view of the Bank of Northern Montana building, later used as the telegraph office. In 1890, this bank changed its name to Stockmen's National Bank and constructed the two-story brick building on the corner.

BANK BLOCK, 1940. This scene shows extensive change in the same block from right to left: the World War I doughboy statue, the Chouteau County Bank in the old Stockmen's building; Leonard H. Morrow's Benton Drugs; Jeff Morger's Bar; the Safeway Grocery; Fred Scarlet's Gambles Store; the Louther Funeral Home in the old Gans and Klein building; and Davis Brother's Grocery Store.

61

OVERLAND BLOCK, 1910. These scenes, taken by Hildore C. Eklund from the Grand Union, show Front Street looking north; River Park is on the right with the Fire Engine House and the bridge. On the left of both photographs is the three-story New Overland Hotel, constructed by John T. Sneath in the spring of 1899 on the site of Fort Benton's first hotel, built in 1866 by Jacob W. Schmidt. Legend has it that during the rebuilding, dirt under the floors of the old hotel and the adjoining Wells Fargo Office was panned, yielding a major amount of gold dust from the placer mining days when gold was weighed out to pay for shipments, rooms, or drinks.

OVERLAND BLOCK, 1920S. This real–photo postcard from 1917 looks north to show in the center the *Chouteau County Independent* newspaper office; to the right are the Pastime Bar, Frank Morger's Saloon, and the New Overland Hotel. The New Overland was a major historic loss when it and adjoining buildings were destroyed by fire in 1949. (Courtesy of Tom Mulvaney.)

OVERLAND BLOCK, 1940. This scene shows the Overland Block in 1940 looking north. In the foreground is a World War I memorial. From left to right are Charles Lepley's Central Service, the Pastime Bar, Earl Morger's Farmers Insurance, the New Overland Hotel and café; Ed's Butcher Shop; the Palace Bar; Dr. J. Kaulbach's Drug Store; Frank Lell's Bakery; W. G. Woodward's Clothing Store; D. G. Lockwood's Drug Store; Joseph Sullivan's Saddlery; and the Benton State Bank building.

OVERLAND BLOCK, 1910s–1920s. These views looking south up Front Street from the Benton State Bank show the following businesses: Benton State Bank; Joseph Sullivan's Saddlery; D. G. Lockwood's Drug Store; Sharp Brother's Grocery; Frank Lell's Bakery; Dr. J. Kaulbach's Drug Store; the Palace Bar; Ed's Butcher Shop; and the New Overland Hotel. The Benton State Bank rode in on the wave of the homestead boom and failed in late 1922, the first of an avalanche of bank failures resulting from inflated land values and drought. The bank was able to pay less than 40 percent of its obligations. The homestead boom was turning to bust. Many farmers who had borrowed more than they thought the land was worth simply walked off and left their homesteads. The hardiest saw it through, and many of their descendants are on the farms today.

CULBERTSON HOUSE BLOCK, 1920S–1930S. The view above shows the historic Pacific Hotel, built in 1882 on the site of the 1876 Centennial Hotel. In 1910, the Pacific Hotel was remodeled and renamed the Culbertson House after owner Robert S. Culbertson, nephew of founder Alexander Culbertson. Businesses during the 1920s and 1930s are, from left to right, the Culbertson House with M. B. Casey Grocery; Japanese descent Tommy Matsumoto's Club Café; Arnold Westfall's Saddlery, later Young's Insurance; Sonny Maloney's Tobacco Shop; McGraw's Saloon, later Capitol Theater; African American Peter Burnett's Shoe Repair; and Coatesworth's Board of Trade Saloon, later a grocery. Chinese proprietors earlier owned Matsumoto's building and conducted an opium den in the basement. A robust Chinese community developed in the 1870s and remained until 1923. Tommy Masumoto later founded the popular Club Cafeteria in Great Falls. During the wild and woolly days of the 1860s, this block earned the infamous reputation as the "bloodiest block in the West." (Above, courtesy of OHRC.)

CHOTEAU HOUSE BLOCK. The view above looks north down Front Street with sheepman Arthur E. McLeish's home partially visible on the left. This home was built on the site of the famed I. G. Baker and Company store. From left to right, other buildings are the Isaac G. Baker home, the Choteau House, and the Hans J. Wackerlin and Company store. Baker came to Fort Benton in 1864 to take over the American Fur Company. In 1866, Baker built an adobe-and-log home next to his store. This oldest surviving home is preserved today, with portions of the original adobe and log walls visible within a wood frame house. The view below looks south up Front Street with the river and bridge on the left and the Choteau House on the right. (Above, courtesy of OHRC; below, courtesy of Tom Mulvaney.)

Five

CHICAGO OF THE PLAINS
HISTORIC BUILDINGS,
COLORFUL CHARACTERS

HISTORIC BUILDINGS. This undivided-back postcard from 1909 samples seven scenes and fine buildings constructed in Fort Benton during the 1880s and 1890s. Clockwise from the lower left, these scenes include St. Clare Hospital, Main (Front) Street looking west, Immaculate Conception Catholic Church, First Methodist Church, St. Paul's Episcopal Church, Main (Front) Street looking east, and the Choteau House. (Photographs by Charles E. Morris, Chinook, Montana.)

THOMAS C. POWER. In 1867, Thomas C. Power stepped off the steamboat *Yorktown* onto the Fort Benton levee with a tiny stock of merchandise. Thomas, with his brother John, expanded rapidly into the Blackfoot robe trade, merchandising, steamboating, and overland freighting. Thomas C. Power parlayed his meager beginnings into a mercantile empire, a seat in the U.S. Senate, and a noteworthy place in Montana and Canadian history.

THOMAS C. POWER BLOCK, 1910. Buildings, from right to left, are Thomas C. Power and Brother Mercantile, Hans J. Wackerlin Hardware; Power Dry Goods; the Power Saddlery; and the Choteau House. Power Mercantile burned in January 1916, and by August, a new store opened. After Power's death in 1923, the statewide Power interests declined and went into bankruptcy in 1934. Before then, in January 1933, manager Jacob Ritter with other local businessmen bought the Fort Benton store and reopened it as the Pioneer Mercantile.

X. Beidler. Colorful, fearless John Xelpho "X" Beidler served as chief hangman for the vigilantes in the gold rush Montana Territory. Later, as a deputy U.S. marshal, Beidler frequently visited Fort Benton, often going down the Missouri to capture lawbreakers and bringing his prisoners back on steamboats. Beidler spun many a yarn on the streets and in the saloons of Fort Benton. (Courtesy of OHRC.)

Charlie Russell and Friends. Until his death in 1926, cowboy artist Charles M. Russell often visited his friends in Fort Benton. This image shows Charlie in the center by the steps of the Benton State Bank with friends saddler Joseph Sullivan (standing at left), visiting artist Edward Borein (facing Russell), rancher Julius Bechard (on the right), and an unidentified man. (Courtesy of OHRC.)

GRAND COURTHOUSE. On the night of January 5, 1883, fire started in the Eagle Bird saloon, owned by African American William Foster. The fire spread rapidly next door to the wooden county courthouse, destroying many records. James Willard Schultz paints a colorful account of the fire, quoting fireman Keno Bill: "Nothin' strange about it. Some records in it just nat'rally had to be destroyed to keep certain fellers I know out of a heap of trouble." While this makes a good story, the charge of arson was never proven. The county moved quickly to build the classic brick courthouse that opened in mid-1884. These photographs were taken in early 1900, and the postcard below served as a souvenir at Minar's store. The building to the left of the courthouse was the county jail. (Below, courtesy of Tom Mulvaney.)

THE PICKET FENCE. The above postcard looks west and shows the main entrance to the new courthouse. Photographer Charles E. Morris dramatically posed four men in front of a white iron picket fence bordering the grounds. Many criticized the fence as an unnecessary expenditure when it was installed in the early 1890s. This kept the fence from having necessary upkeep, and it was eventually removed. Local merchants George W. Crane and D. G. Lockwood published the above postcard for distribution in their stores. The real-photo postcard below shows the south side of the new courthouse and the county jail. (Above, photograph by Charles E. Morris, Chinook, Montana.)

THE COURTHOUSE TODAY.
These real-photo postcards
show the classic Queen Anne
architecture of the courthouse.
Gus Senieur, an early Fort
Benton contractor, designed
the building, which is located
on Franklin Street in the heart
of Fort Benton. Senieur and
the firm of Kees and Fish built
the courthouse using brick
manufactured at Fort Benton.
Chouteau County commissioners
have long committed to the
continued use and maintenance of
this historic building, and it was
added to the National Register
of Historic Places in 1980. This
courthouse is the second oldest
in Montana in use today.

COUNTY JAIL. The old Chouteau County Jail, built in 1881 just west of the courthouse, was designed by James Warwick and constructed by John R. Wilton. The above scene shows the brick jail shortly after completion with Sheriff John J. Healy in the center. The other two men are unidentified. Colorful Johnny Healy cut a wide swath across frontier Montana as an adventurer, journalist, storyteller, lawman, and whiskey trader. Fort Benton legend says the jail was constructed by then-Sheriff Healy, but residents so resented the luxurious quarters for prisoners they failed to renominate Healy. The image below shows the aging, deteriorating jail in more recent years, after it was added to the National Register of Historic Places. This historic old jail was destroyed in 1994 and was replaced by a larger law enforcement and human services facility across the street. (Above, courtesy of OHRC; below, courtesy of Karen Bryant.)

OLD ENGINE HOUSE. Fort Benton, like all frontier towns, faced the threat of fire. In 1883, contractor John Wilton built the Fire Engine House on the river levee. Engine Company No. 1 organized, held drills and social balls, and waited for a hand pumper to arrive by steamboat from St. Louis. The pumper was off-loaded downriver at Cow Island, and when it finally arrived, it had a wheel missing and paint pealing. The Engine House served many years as the firehouse. The south side of the building became the Fort Benton City Hall until 1966. In 1975, the Engine House was restored, and it was added to the National Register of Historic Places in 1980. Today the building houses and displays the original fire equipment while the south side serves as the Fort Benton Visitor Center. (Below, courtesy of Karen Bryant.)

What does this mean to you.

St. Paul's Episcopal Church. The Episcopal church came to the Montana Territory in 1867 with Bishop Daniel S. Tuttle, who rode a circuit to mining camps and frontier posts on horseback. An abandoned saloon, later a hotel and school, housed Bishop Tuttle's first service in Fort Benton. When Rev. S. C. Blackiston arrived in 1879, a committee was named by Bishop Tuttle to build a new church. Architect and contractor John Wilton built this historic church in the Norman–Gothic style in 1880, and the first service was held on August 10, 1881. The above undivided-back postcard, postmarked in 1906, bears the intriguing comment below the photograph, "What does this mean to you?" The postcard below, photographed several years later, shows the addition of an ornate white iron fence. (Below, photograph by Charles E. Morris, Chinook, Montana.)

The Episcopal Church, Fort Benton, Mont.

St. Paul's Church Today. The church name came from St. Paul's School in Concord, New Hampshire, the home of visiting headmaster Rev. ? Colt, who made the initial contribution. Other contributors of the $4,000 subscription read like a who's who among Fort Benton businessmen in the 1880s: William G. Conrad, J. S. Hill, William H. Todd, A. B. Kester, Ferdinand C. Roosevelt, Charles Conrad, Charles Duer, Winfield S. Wetzel, Joseph A. Baker, and Paris Gibson. St. Paul's is the oldest church in Fort Benton and the oldest surviving Episcopal church in Montana. St. Paul's was added to the National Register of Historic Places in 1980 and today continues to serve a small congregation. (Below, courtesy of Karen Bryant.)

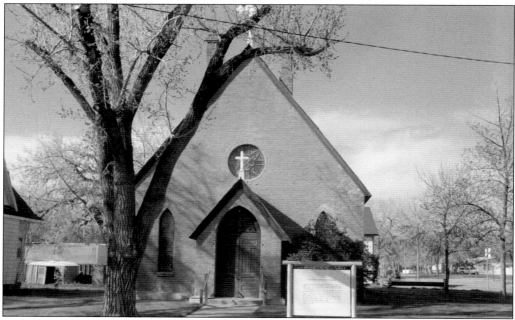

IMMACULATE CHURCH. The first religious service in the area was held by Fr. Jean Pierre DeSmet at Fort Lewis on September 27, 1846, in the presence of Fr. Nicholas Point. Over the years, the famed "Black Robe" Father DeSmet and other Catholic priests visiting Fort Benton performed weddings, baptisms, and services. Most of the Engages at the fort were Catholic. These postcards show the second Church of the Immaculate Conception, which replaced the first church in 1906. The above postcard, postmarked 1910, shows the rebuilt stone Immaculate Church and bears an intriguing note on the back from Mrs. Isaac M. Rogers: "This is the picture of the church I told you that frightened me so." The card below, sent in 1910, notes "They also have a large Catholic Sanitarium [hospital] here and care for about 30 orphan children in one part of the building."

Immaculate Church,

Fort Benton, Mont.

IMMACULATE CHURCH TODAY. In 1878, Fr. Camillus Imoda arrived in Fort Benton and directed the construction of the first Catholic church, making the Catholic congregation the first to build a church. The first wood-frame church burned to the ground on December 31, 1905. In November 1906, construction began on this stone church, which served the parish for 60 years. The bell in the tower is "Michael," a brass bell installed in the first church in 1880. For more than 100 years, this bell called the faithful to services and tolled for fires, celebrations, and disasters. During the flood of 1908, Michael rang all night, leading people to safety from the dark floodwaters of the Missouri flowing through the streets of Fort Benton. (Below, courtesy of Karen Bryant.)

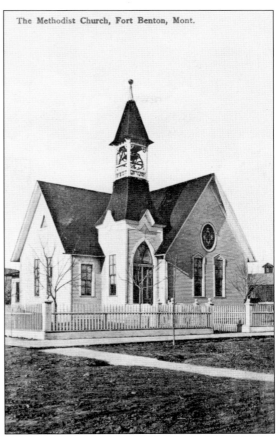

The Methodist Church, Fort Benton, Mont.

BROTHER VAN. The First Methodist Episcopal Church in Fort Benton was built in 1898 by Rev. William W. Van Orsdel. Young "Will" Van Orsdel arrived at Fort Benton on Sunday, June 30, 1872, on the steamboat *Far West*. That first day, he preached the first sermon by a Protestant minister, acquiring the nickname "Brother Van." He was a frequent visitor to Fort Benton, and in March each year before his death in 1919, the church hosted a birthday celebration for Montana's beloved pioneer preacher. The church bell is now in a museum. The postcard below, taken at the First Methodist Church in Valier, Montana, shows circuit-riding Brother Van standing third from the left in the first row with his signature white vest, bow tie, and hat in hand. (Right, photograph by Charles E. Morris; below, courtesy of Tom Mulvaney.)

I wish you were going to this school. Every body is well in Benton including Kehoe. Ben sends his love. Kest regards

R. R. R.

FORT BENTON SCHOOLS. The first brick maker moved to Fort Benton in 1877, and his first bricks built a small school late that year. An early teacher was Helen Clarke, the daughter of Malcolm Clarke, a fur trader whose murder by Blackfeet in 1869 led to the Baker Massacre. By 1879, the new school was crowded with 72 pupils. A 34-by-46-foot addition, built in 1880, eased the problem for a short while. In 1882, the school board wrestled with the problem of whether to admit African American students to the school. Backed by the Lincoln Republican *River Press*, the school board voted to admit black children. Shown in these views is a new three-story school building completed in 1884. The above undivided-back postcard notes: "I wish you were going to this school." (Above, courtesy of Tom Mulvaney.)

HIGH SCHOOL   FT. BENTON, MONT.   'AT MINAR'S.'

SCHOOLS, 1900–1937. The new school was completed in 1884, just as the town population began to decline. The above view of the school in the 1890s shows the grounds bordered by a white picket fence similar to the courthouse across the street. In 1901, a high school was added with a starting enrollment of 17. The homestead boom during the 1910s increased enrollment, and this led to a large addition in 1916. The view below shows the 1884 building on the left, the 1916 addition in the center, and the small 1877 school on the right. The school buildings burned down on August 2, 1937, in one of Fort Benton's most spectacular fires. Tragically, lost in this fire were several display cases with early Fort Benton artifacts.

Fort Benton High School, Fort Benton, Mont.

NEW ELEMENTARY SCHOOL. In early 1937, construction began on a new elementary school with a gymnasium, but it was not ready by the time of the August fire. Classes were held around town until completion of the new school in October. In this view, the high school built the following year appears on the left.

NEW HIGH SCHOOL. After the 1937 fire, the high school shown here was constructed in 1938 on the south side of the new elementary school building with partial funding from the New Deal Works Progress Administration (WPA). Post–World War II increases in enrollment led to the construction of another two-story, brick high school with a gymnasium on the grounds of the old town baseball diamond, opening in the fall of 1958.

THWING HOUSE. Built by I. G. Baker and T. C. Power in the spring of 1868 between their stores, the Thwing House opened on Front Street at a time when there were seven steamboats moored at the levee. This two-story wood-frame structure was lined with adobe and was named for the manager Mrs. Elizabeth H. Thwing. In the early 1870s, the hotel closed but was rented as officers' quarters for the military post with an adobe annex for a saloon. In 1879, Jere Sullivan and J. B. Hill reopened the hotel as the Choteau House. The above postcard-sized blotter shows the Choteau House in the lower right corner as it appeared in 1879. Fire partially destroyed the hotel, and in 1903, Sullivan rebuilt an expanded two-story hotel with a brick front, shown in the postcard below. (Below, photograph by Charles E. Morris, Chinook, Montana.)

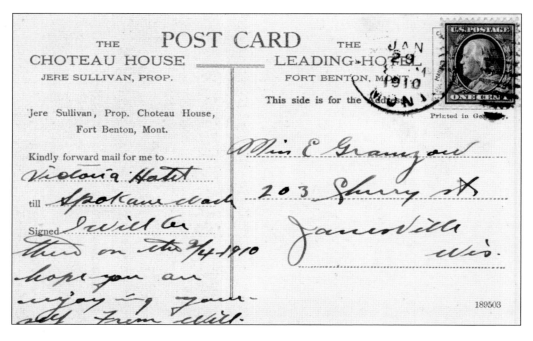

NEW CHOTEAU HOUSE. The expanded Choteau House, with its attractive brick front and new addition with a bar, was advertised in the above postcard as "The Choteau House, Jere Sullivan, Prop. The Leading Hotel" in Fort Benton. During the height of the homestead boom, Jere Sullivan added a third story and changed the name to the New Choteau House. The undivided-back postcard below shows the New Choteau House as it appeared in the 1910s. (Below, photograph by Charles E. Morris, Great Falls.)

NEW CHOTEAU HOUSE INTERIOR. This postcard shows the interior of New Choteau House with its well-appointed lobby and dining room. Jere Sullivan passed on in 1919, leaving Fort Benton "without its ambassador of good-will and Irish Charm," in the words of the *River Press*. Clarence McCauley married Sullivan's widow and ran the Choteau House until 1944. Regrettably, the building has long been abandoned and is today endangered. (Photograph by Charles E. Morris, Great Falls; courtesy of Tom Mulvaney)

BENTON STATE BANK. Built in 1910 at the south corner of Front and St. John Streets, the new Benton State Bank was the first new commercial establishment in many years. The two-story bank was built of light-colored brick. The bank failed and closed its doors on December 26, 1922, paying less than 40 percent of its obligations. During recent years, this fine building has undergone extensive restoration. (Photograph by Hildore C. Eklund)

STOCKMEN'S NATIONAL BANK. The Bank of Northern Montana opened on June 1, 1880, to become Fort Benton's first bank. In a sign of the times during the open-range era, and backed by ranchers of the Shonkin Stock Association, the bank changed its name in 1889 to Stockmen's National Bank. Cattlemen throughout northern Montana carried accounts with Stockmen's, and the bank prospered until the homestead years. Despite the bank's boast in the above postcard that it was "One of the strongest financial institutions in the northwest," it failed in January 1924. Eventually, the bank paid off over 96 percent of its obligations. Later, in 1924, the Square Butte Bank from the tiny town of that name moved to Fort Benton and became the Chouteau County Bank. Today the building houses a restaurant and bar. (Below, photograph by Charles E. Morris.)

St. Claire Hospital, Fort Benton, Mont.

St. Clare Hospital. A public subscription began in 1882 to build a hospital, and by September 1883, construction of a two-story, 86-by-44-foot building began. Although completed in August 1884, occupancy awaited the arrival of Catholic sisters. On July 27, 1886, three Sisters of Charity of Providence, Mother Mary of the Resurrection, Sr. Anna Magnan, and Sr. Mary Wilfred, arrived in Fort Benton to open the hospital. Named for St. Clare of Montefalco, northern Montana's first hospital began admitting patients on August 11, 1886. Several additions were completed over the years until 1952, when a new St. Claire Hospital was built. In December 1974, St. Clare Hospital was turned over to Chouteau County after more than 88 years of operation by the Sisters of Charity. (Below, courtesy of OHRC.)

ST. CLARE HOSPITAL
Fort Benton, Montana
Established in 1886 by
The Sisters of Charity of Providence
Showing 1952 Addition

I. G. BAKER HOUSE. Isaac G. Baker built this home for his wife, Fanny, in 1866. Constructed of rough-sawn lumber and hand-hewn beams, it had adobe brick walls several feet thick. Wood siding and a porch were added in 1876. Among many visitors, Gen. Thomas Francis Meagher ate his last meal there before drowning off a steamboat. Added to the National Register of Historic Places in 1980, this historic building is part of the museums' complex.

W. S. WETZEL HOUSE. In September 1882, contractor Gus Senieur built an elegant, brick, two-and-a-half-story "mansion on the hill" for Winfield Scott Wetzel, a merchant and early trader. Within two years, Wetzel was bankrupt, the victim of his own generosity, and banker Charles E. Duer bought the mansion. Sent as a New Year's greeting on December 28, 1906, this real-photo postcard shows the Wetzel home with its carriage house on the right.

224-Fort Benton (Mont.) Sanitarium.

FORT BENTON SANITARIUM. The Wetzel/Duer mansion had a distinctive three–and–a–half-story cupola with gabled dormers in its pyramid roof. A large copper weather vane from the old fort crowned the roof. From the cupola, the entire town and valley could be surveyed. In 1910, Dr. Enoch M. Porter opened the Fort Benton Sanitarium in the mansion. The sanitarium operated as a hospital and housed tuberculosis patients until 1916, when it closed. Only the carriage house survives today as a residence. Dr. Porter moved to Great Falls in 1917 and, with three other doctors, founded the Great Falls Clinic. (Both, courtesy of Tom Mulvaney.)

FORT BENTON SANITARIUM.

GREEN'S OPERA HOUSE. This two-story brick structure was built in 1882 as the Masonic temple. Over the years, this building housed Sharp's Grocery and other businesses on the lower level and today has the Benton Pharmacy. During the 1890s and early 1900s, the second floor served as Green's Opera House. Added to the National Register of Historic Places in 1980, this building is the only surviving venue in Montana where the 1904 Fort Shaw girls played basketball games. (Courtesy of OHRC.)

GIRLS' BASKETBALL TEAM. In the spring of 1904, before Fort Benton schools began playing basketball, the Fort Shaw Indian School girls' basketball team played the first game of basketball in Fort Benton at Green's Opera House. The Fort Shaw team gained fame later that year as Montana champions and for winning their games against all comers at the 1904 St. Louis World's Fair.

THOMAS C. POWER AND BROTHER LUMBER COMPANY. In 1910, Thomas C. Power and Brother opened an implement dealership and a lumber company to capture part of the new homestead business. The lumber shed was 88 feet by 110 feet with a capacity of about 800,000 feet of lumber and other building materials. The postcard shows the new lumber company shortly after its completion, with advertising printed in the correspondence section.

BENTON STABLES. Owner Hilare C. LaBarre opened the Benton Stables in the early 1900s. This postcard shows LaBarre with his favorite silky trotting horse. The homestead boom fueled major growth in Fort Benton for the first time in two decades. Horses, wagons, blacksmith shops, and stables were in high demand. Benton Railworks occupied the building on the left. (Courtesy of Tom Mulvaney.)

C. C. GRANT GENERAL BLACKSMITHING. Another businessman taking advantage of the homestead boom, Cady C. Grant opened his blacksmith and wagon repair store in 1909. Located on Front Street on the upper levee opposite Davis Grocery, this blacksmith shop only lasted a couple of years. (Courtesy of Tom Mulvaney.)

CHOUTEAU COUNTY FREE LIBRARY. Under Dorothy McLeish and the Fort Benton's Women's Club, the first county public library in Montana opened in Fort Benton in 1916. Two years later, the library moved into a new building designed by Helena architect George H. Carsley, built by contractor James Sherry, and funded by the Carnegie Foundation. This postcard shows the Chouteau County Free Library, an early Carnegie library in Montana.

FRATERNITY HALL. To the right of the library is Fraternity Hall, built originally as a four-story brick building for Fort Benton's first newspaper, the *Benton Record*, which was published from 1875 to 1884. In 1929, the building was stuccoed and the upper floor removed. Tragically, in cleaning out the upper floor, a treasure trove of glass negatives was hauled to the city dump, destroying the invaluable record of Fort Benton's premier photographer, Daniel Dutro. (Courtesy of OHRC.)

FORT BENTON SWIMMING POOL. Fort Benton got a public swimming pool in 1936 but at a heavy cost. The WPA demolished the old Isaac G. Baker Company wool warehouse to make room for the pool. In the process, most of the historic records of the Isaac G. Baker Company stored in the warehouse were hauled to the city dump and tragically lost to history.

FORT BENTON MUSEUM. The school fire of 1937 destroyed display cases of valuable historic artifacts. In 1958, the Fort Benton Museum was dedicated, one of the first community museums in Montana. The success of this museum led to its expansion in 1965 and a new name, the Museum of the Upper Missouri. Today this pioneer of Fort Benton's four museums celebrates Fort Benton's colorful history with "20 Tall Tales of the Upper Missouri."

PROUD MILITARY TRADITION. From the 1860s, Chouteau County has had a proud military tradition. Seven distinguished admirals and general officers attended Fort Benton schools, an exceptional record for a small town. Foremost among these hometown leaders is Adm. Ulysses S. Grant Sharp, commander of the U.S. Pacific Fleet from 1964 to 1968. This image shows the officers' quarters at the Fort Benton Military Post. Built of adobe around 1869, this historic building stands as a residence today.

Six

Two Historic Gems
Grand Union and
Fort Benton Bridge

JEWEL IN THE CROWN. The jewel in Fort Benton's crown is the Grand Union Hotel, both the oldest operating hotel and among the most important historic structures in Montana. This cyanotype-processed undivided-back postcard from 1906 shows the Grand Union nestled on the steamboat levee at the south edge of River Park. Visible in the foreground is stonework built in the 1890s along the levee to stabilize the waterfront.

THE GRAND UNION, 1900. Built in 1882 with Victorian Renaissance architecture at the height of the steamboat era, the Grand Union welcomed weary travelers to spend a few nights in its luxury before they set out to less "civilized places" like Virginia City and points west. Furnished with Victorian appointments, the dining room's silver service, white linen, and Bavarian china served the rich and famous.

The Grand Union Hotel, Fort Benton, Mont.

"THE GRANDEST AFFAIR." An elegant ladies' parlor on the second floor with a private stairway to the dining room saved the ladies from exposure to the rowdy crowd in the saloon and poker rooms. The ornate lobby desk and broad black walnut staircase highlight the fine carpentry work throughout. The opening ball for the Grand Union was proclaimed by the *Benton Record* as, "the grandest affair of its kind ever witnessed in Benton, and most probably in the Territory."

Grand Union Hotel, Fort Benton, Mont.

TODD HAD A DREAM. At the height of the steamboat era in 1879, William H. Todd had a dream. Fort Benton was booming with thousands of passengers and tons of freight arriving at the head of navigation. Todd was more than talk, and in 1880, the Benton Hotel Company formed, local bricks were ordered, and, in August 1881, ground was broken. Thomas Tweedy served as architect and contractor, and Frank Coombs supervised the brickwork.

GRAND AND UNION. "Grand Union" fit the post–Civil War times. The architectural character of the three-story hotel is unique, with bricks carefully fitted into bold decorations, extensive corbelling, wrought-iron balconies, and ornate chimneys. Whitman Gibson "Vinegar" Jones, a master carpenter, built the elaborate lobby counter and cashier's cage, the grand walnut staircase leading to the second floor, and the exceptional interior woodwork throughout. (Courtesy of Tom Mulvaney)

VIEW FROM BOND STREET. This view from 1917 looks east toward the Missouri River and its bluffs with the Stockman's Bank on the right and a ladies' millinery store on the left. The Grand Union's entrance was on Bond Street, and the ladies' entrance was on Front Street. The main entrance was located in the lobby with the dining room on the left and the saloon on the right. The hotel did well during the homestead boom years of the 1910s.

OF MANY LIVES. During its 127 years, the Grand Union has had many lives. It has been the most luxurious hotel between St. Louis and Seattle. It has been a run-of-the-mill hotel, and it has been a virtual flophouse with rooms to rent for two bits. Despite its placement in 1976 on the National Register of Historic Places, the hotel suffered years of derelict closure, with interior furnishings sold at auction.

THE JEWEL RETURNS. Today the grand old lady of Montana hotels shines brightly, restored to its golden-era glory with modernity carefully folded in. Under owners James and Cheryl Gagnon, the Grand Union has been restored and is in business. The Grand Union is one of Montana's greatest preservation success stories. (Courtesy of Karen Bryant.)

GRAND UNION CHRISTMAS. When the Grand Union opened in November 1882, fine dining and service came from head chef Alex Martin and 10 other African Americans comprising all but two of the hotel staff. Christmas on the frontier was a community affair, a time for celebration with dining and dancing. This painting by Brian Morger shows a wintry Christmas at the Grand Union Hotel. (Courtesy of James and Cheryl Gagnon.)

FIRST BRIDGE. With the end of the steamboat era, Fort Benton merchants looked for ways to built their transportation base and capture the lucrative cattle and wool business in Judith Basin. A bridge was needed to replace ferries across the Missouri River. Public subscription raised money, and in January 1888, contracts were let to the Milwaukee Bridge and Iron Works. The architectural firm Ryane and Henry designed three truss spans of 175 feet each, a small span of 65 feet, and a swinging span of 225 feet. The bridge opened in mid-December 1888 at a cost of $60,000. The swing span was opened for only two steamboats, the *O.K.* and the *Josephine*, and the great flood of 1908 destroyed the span. Both images show the bridge after the swing span was replaced by a fixed wooden span.

THE FORT BENTON BRIDGE. Privately funded, the Fort Benton bridge was the first across the Missouri River in Montana, the first all-steel truss bridge, and the oldest steel bridge in Montana. It was a toll bridge operated by a private company until it was sold for $9,999 to Choteau County in 1896. This real-photo postcard looks west across the bridge toward the town.

FORT BENTON BRIDGE, 1934. The bridge is visible in the distance in this image. Contractor Frank Coombs built the two-story brick home in the foreground for ferry operator and freighter Edward L. Smith.

HISTORIC WALKING BRIDGE. In 1963, a new bridge, paid for by federal and county funds, replaced the historic Fort Benton bridge. Fortunately the first bridge across the Missouri River was preserved and added to National Register of Historic Places in 1980. Since 1982, the Fort Benton bridge has served as a walking bridge with a spectacular view of Fort Benton and both up and down the Missouri River. (Below, courtesy of Karen Bryant.)

Seven

VENICE ON THE MISSOURI
THE GREAT FLOOD OF 1908

FORT BENTON AS VENICE. During the great flood on the Upper Missouri in June 1908, the streets of Fort Benton flowed like rivers. After days of rain and melting snowpack, the Missouri River became a torrent. Failure of the Hauser Dam and then the Black Eagle Dam at Great Falls sent a tide of water cascading toward Fort Benton. By the time the crest reached Fort Benton, the swell overflowed the riverbanks near the present-day fairgrounds.

Looking North on Main Street, Fort Benton, Mont.
During Flood of 1908

FRONT STREET UNDERWATER. The river followed its ancient channel down Franklin Street rather than coming over the levee along Front Street. By early evening on June 5th, water flowed through many streets and houses. Water was 6 feet deep around the courthouse, just two blocks from the levee, but it only lapped at the doorsteps of the Grand Union Hotel and the New Overland Hotel. The next morning, Front and Main Streets looked like canals in Venice.

TAKING TO BOATS. Residents retreated to higher ground, loading themselves and their valuable possessions in boats or canoes, or dragging them in any conveyance they could find. Through early darkness created by overcast rainy skies, the Michael bell rang out, directing all to safety on the hill behind the Church of the Immaculate Conception.

Looking South on Main Street, Fort Benton, Mont.
During Flood of 1908

GREATEST OF THREE FLOODS. The June 1908 flood was the greatest Fort Benton had ever seen, but it was not the only one. A rise in the Missouri in June 1876 caused some overflow of the river at Fort Benton. An ice gorge formed just below town on February 24, 1884, and put 3 feet of water on Front Street.

RAGING RIVER. For 20 years, the great 225-foot turn span at the Fort Benton Bridge stood ready to swing open for the steamboats that never came. The swing span had opened only for two boats, the *O.K.* and the *Josephine* on pleasure tours. The big span went down due to the raging Missouri River in the flood on June 6, 1908.

GREATEST LOSS. Floodwaters undermined the round center pier of the swing span. The river flow caught its decking and twisted it around the pier like matchsticks. The breaking metal emitted showers of sparks, making a weird scene in the darkness. The entire superstructure fell into the river with a crash that was spectacular.

HIGH WATER MARK. By Saturday evening, June 6th, the volume and current of the river reached its crest and extended the submerged district. By Sunday morning, the water began to subside, and the big clean up began. No one had been lost to the floodwaters, but the town's wooden sidewalks had disappeared downriver, and the bridge was out of action. (Courtesy of OHRC.)

BACK TO FERRIES. Shortly after the flood, ferries returned to the Fort Benton levee for the first time in 20 years for conveyance across the Missouri River. Ferries operated until early 1909, when a new wooden span was completed. The large house in the background is the Edward L. Smith/Ben Woodcock home.

SUSPENSION FOOTBRIDGE. A precarious suspension footbridge closed the gap between the shore and the second span for a short time. A sign above the footbridge warned "This bridge is for foot passengers only. $5.00 Fine for standing or moving faster than a walk." The wreckage of the swing span and pier cluttered the river.

TEMPORARY MEASURES. The suspension footbridge and ferries served the river crossing as temporary measures. Heavier traffic could cross the river only during low water at the ford just downriver from the bridge. In March 1909, a new wooden span was completed to reopen the bridge just eight months after the disaster. In 1927, a new steel truss replaced the temporary wooden span to hold heavier vehicular traffic. The historic Fort Benton bridge closed in 1963, replaced by the new federal/county-funded Chouteau County Bridge upriver.

Eight

FROM BISON TO BEEF AND WHEAT
AGRICULTURAL ERA

THE OPEN-RANGE ERA. As bison herds were decimated and faded from Montana's open spaces, cattle took their place. The open-range cattle ranching era lasted for some 30 years, from the late 1870s to the early 1900s. Wide-open ranges extended from the Musselshell Valley to southern Alberta and from the Sun River Valley to the Milk River. Vast herds in the thousands established Montana as one of the leading beef sources of the nation.

THE ROUNDUP #2. No one better captured the open-range era than Charles M. Russell. He had been a horse wrangler, night herder, trapper, and sheepherder before becoming a full-time artist in 1893. Cattle ranged openly across the broad landscape in every direction from Fort Benton. Annually the Shonkin, Sun River, and North Montana Stock Associations rounded up their cattle, branded the calves, and shipped cattle to eastern markets.

M 229 A beef herd watering at a lake

THE CATTLEMEN. Open-range pioneers Milton E. Milner, Adkinson W. Kingsbury, Robert Coburn, Joseph A. Baker, John Lepley, Daniel A. G. Floweree, Charles E. Conrad, John Harris, and others based their operations in Fort Benton. The vast open range saw herd sizes in the tens of thousands, as shown in this photograph by Charles E. Morris. Ranchers shipped their cattle by the new railroads and built fine homes on their ranches and in Fort Benton.

DINNER ON THE RANGE. With his chuck wagon and supplies, the camp cook, or "cookie," followed the herd, having midday dinner ready for large roundup crews such as the 14 men in this crew in this photograph by Charles E. Morris. Cowboys and their wives and sweethearts formed the heart of the open range cattle industry, riding the range, wrangling the horses, standing night herd, cooking the food, and keeping the operation going.

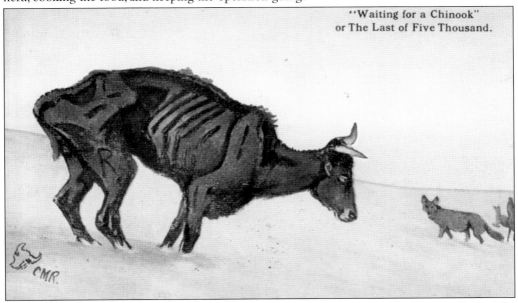

"Waiting for a Chinook"
or The Last of Five Thousand.

WAITING FOR A CHINOOK. During the winter of 1886–1887, cowboy Charlie Russell cared for a herd of thousands of cattle for cattlemen Louis Stadler and Louis Kaufman. Severe late-winter storms devastated the herd, and Stadler and Kaufman grew concerned. In response to their queries, Russell wrote no words but instead painted this scene, known as *The Last of the Five Thousand*, that told the whole story.

IN MONTANA. A PRIZE BAND OF SHEEP. COPYRIGHT 1907

RAISING SHEEP. One result of cattle losses during the open-range era was the introduction of vast herds of sheep. Some northern Montana ranchers like Ole G. Osnes shifted to sheep, while others keep herds of both sheep and cattle on separate ranges. The classic sight of the sheepherder, with his band of sheep, horse, wagon, and dog, became commonplace. (Below, photograph by Charles E. Morris, Chinook, Montana.)

A Western Shepherd and his Flock

SHEEP TO MARKET. These undivided-back postcards from the early 1900s show two scenes. The above scene, taken from a balcony of the Grand Union Hotel, shows a large band of sheep on Front Street in Fort Benton. The scene below shows a wagon loaded with wool coming to market over the Fort Benton bridge. There was a major eastern market, and both sheep and wool were shipped by rail in large quantities from Fort Benton. (Above, photograph by Walter B. Dean, courtesy of Tom Mulvaney.)

337 B. Load of Wool Coming to Market at Fort Benton, Montana. Geo. W. Crane, Publisher.

113

GREETINGS FROM
FORT BENTON, MONTANA

A178

TODAY'S RANCHES. The long-term effect of overgrazing the range, as well as tough winters, led to major changes in the 1890s. These changes accelerated in the early 1900s as large sections of northern Montana opened to homesteading. The grand era of open–range ranching came to an end, but cattle ranching continued. Today's ranches with fences, extensive haying operations, and branding in corrals rather than in the open still provide the nation with Montana beef. In addition, the ranching and cowboy tradition continue with rodeos and horse racing throughout northern Montana each summer. (Left, photograph by Charles E. Morris, Great Falls.)

Greetings from FORT BENTON "Birthplace of Montana"

PRAIRIE FRIENDS, 1908–1920. This 72-by-32-inch oil mural by Robert F. Morgan hangs in the Montana Agricultural Center. Morgan depicted a homesteader's wife and young daughter feeding chickens and enjoying a pet sheep and a fawn antelope while the homesteader plowed the ground. (Photograph by John Godwyn; courtesy of River and Plains Society.)

COWBOY'S FAREWELL. This postcard from Fort Benton was popular around 1910 with its theme "The Cowboy's Farewell to the Dry-Land Farmer." The two photographs are "Cowboys Packing up to Leave the Range" and "Dry Land Farmer Breaking up the Virgin Soil." The cowboy in the poem laments "I've been all my life in the saddle. / All I know is to rope an old cow. / And I never could work on a sheep ranch— / And I'm damned if I'll follow a plow."

ENTER THE HOMESTEADER. The Enlarged 1909 Homestead Act allowed 320-acre claims, and extensive promotion by the Great Northern Railroad triggered a Montana land rush. Men, families, and single women arrived by train. This card shows homesteaders with hired "locators" and carriages setting out to visit the location of their new claims. In the 1910s, it commonly cost $20 to hire the services of a locator.

THRESHING GRAIN. The first years of homesteading in Chouteau County featured horse-drawn plows breaking ground and seeding wheat, oats, rye, and other crops. Once the grain was ripe, it was cut, gathered, threshed, and hauled to market, all with horses. Often a large threshing crew moved around the country in operations like that shown in this scene.

The Homesteaders Cabin on the Claim, Montana.

ON THE CLAIM. Their claims located, homesteaders built crude claim shacks and went to work in their fields and homes. The above postcard shows a homestead couple with their daughter by their first home on the land. This postcard, published by the Great Northern Railway, was designed for the homesteader to send home and gives instructions for obtaining a "free illustrated book on Montana." The scene below shows a common sight in the homestead era: women homesteaders in their claim shack. Single or widowed women were allowed to file claims, and many did, so many that east of Fort Benton a community informally known as "Ladyville" was formed by six women homesteaders. Many homesteaders came, but fewer stayed. The wet years of the mid-1910s turned to dry years toward the end of the decade, and the term "free land, no guarantee" became all too true.

Holding Down a Claim in the West.

The Aultman-Taylor Gas Tractor has many uses. Here this one is at work building a railroad near Ft. Benton, Montana. There's always work for an Aultman-Taylor. 18292

HOPE AND OPPORTUNITY. Farming progressed from horse-drawn equipment to mechanization. The above postcard from 1914 advertises "The Aultman-Taylor Gas Tractor has many uses. Here this one is at work building a railroad near Ft. Benton, Montana." Shown below is the 5-millionth International Harvester tractor, produced in 1974 and now displayed at the Museum of the Northern Great Plains. Homesteading involved hardships difficult to imagine today. Setting off into a harsh landscape was the first of many challenges. Some hoped for a better life in an occupation for which they were ill prepared. Over time, about 25 percent survived and succeeded, but some 75 percent failed, lost their land, and moved on. Today's farmers are largely descended from the hardy first-generation homesteaders who held down their debt in bad times, tenaciously worked hard, and acquired more land in good times.

Nine

REMEMBERING THE PAST
CELEBRATING FORT BENTON HISTORY

HISTORICAL SIGNS. For many years, travel signs have been in place along U.S. Highway 89 between Great Falls and Havre on the western bluffs overlooking the Missouri River and Fort Benton to lure travelers. Fort Benton's location off the major interstate highways and away from Glacier and Yellowstone parks detracts from large-scale tourism. This sign from the 1950s emphasized the steamboat era, the fur trade era, and Fort Benton as "the Birthplace of Montana."

FORT BENTON ROUNDUP, 1913. The North Montana Roundup Association held many annual meetings at Fort Benton from the days of the open range, but none outdid the celebration on April 22, 1913. A special train and 36 automobiles brought more than 200 people from Great Falls, including the Black Eagle Band. As the train arrived at the depot, it was "held up" in the old fashion with the leader of the desperadoes being Sheriff Isaac M. Rogers. Shots were fired, and the "victims" were made to disembark and march to town. The above real–photo postcard shows the enactment of the holdup welcoming the visitors to town. The scene below shows the Fort Benton and Black Eagle Bands parading down Front Street. After a noon dinner, a rodeo was held, followed by a band concert and an evening dance at the Baker Opera House.

Chouteau County Fair. Since 1913, the Chouteau County Fair has highlighted ranching and farming agricultural traditions. The fairgrounds on the south edge of Fort Benton featured a rodeo, horse racing, and community displays of crops and livestock. This real–photo postcard shows rider Bennie Thompson winning one of the horse races at the 1915 Chouteau County Fair. (Courtesy of Tom Mulvaney.)

World War I. Many from Chouteau County served in World War I, and on Armistice Day, November 11, 1923, the *Spirit of American Doughboy Monument* was dedicated in Fort Benton to commemorate their service. This 7-foot statue, sculpted by Ernest Moore Viquesney, is one of very few in Montana. Its original location on Front Street beside the Grand Union led late night drivers to collisions, so it was relocated to Veterans Park.

SHEP, FOREVER FAITHFUL. In 1936, a sheepherder died at St. Clare Hospital and was shipped to his home by train. Little noticed at the time, a shepherd dog followed the casket to the station. During the next 5 years, Shep met passenger trains at the Fort Benton station to greet his returning master. Ed Shields, a Great Northern conductor, with station agent Anthony V. Schanche and section foreman Patrick McSweeney, pieced the story together, and by 1939, Shep was international news. Shep became a celebrity for passengers on arriving trains, and many bought Shep story booklets, with the benefits going to the Montana State School for the Deaf and Blind.

"SHEP, ED SHIELDS AND A.V. SCHANCHE

Impressive Memorial, Fort Benton, Mont.—B 810

ETERNAL SHEP. On January 12, 1942, an aged Shep slipped on an icy rail and was struck by an arriving train. More than 200 people attended Shep's funeral as the mayors of Great Falls and Fort Benton, a Boy Scout Honor Guard, and pallbearers trudged along the trail leading to his grave on the bluffs overlooking the Fort Benton Station. The above scene shows Shep's grave site with a small obelisk and a painted cutout of Shep. In 1994, Fort Benton dedicated a bronze statue of Shep by Bob Scriver on the levee just north of the Grand Union. This larger-than-life statue is shown in the postcard below with the river in the background. The enduring story of Shep is still being told in books, articles, and songs around the world.

ST. LOUIS BENTON BOAT RACE. In 1937, just before completion of the Fort Peck Dam and the permanent closing of the Missouri River to navigation, a St. Louis–to–Fort Benton motor cruiser race was held to commemorate the steamboat era. This event-of-the-year race ended on June 19 to the cheers of an immense crowd of more than 12,000. The above view shows the winning Glasgow–Fort Peck boat crossing the finish line at the end of the 2,300-mile race. A large encampment of Blackfeet formed at the fairgrounds, reminiscent of fur trade days. In the view below, the Blackfeet lead the Missouri River Steamboat Days Parade. Over the years, Fort Benton has had many other celebrations—its centennial in 1946, the U.S. Bicentennial in 1976, and others—but none topped the massive crowds at the boat race. (Courtesy of OHRC.)

Bibliography

Bryant, Karen, compiler. *Historical Signs of Fort Benton*. Fort Benton, MT: Karen's Insta-print Studio, 1998.

Fort Benton *River Press*. "Grand Union Hotel's 125 Anniversary Edition." November, 2, 2007.

Hanchett, Leland J., Jr. *Montana's Benton Road*. Wolf Creek, MT: Pine Run Publishing, 2008.

Historical Fort Benton, Montana Established 1846. Big Sandy, MT: The Mountaineer, 1976.

Lass, William G. *Navigating the Missouri: Steamboating on Nature's Highway, 1819–1935*. Norman, OK: The Arthur H. Clark Company, 2008.

Lepley, John G. *Birthplace of Montana: A History of Fort Benton*. Missoula, MT: Pictorial Histories Publishing Company, 1999.

———. *Blackfeet Fur Trade on the Upper Missouri*. Missoula, MT: Pictorial Histories Publishing Company, 2004.

———. *Luxury on the Levee*. Self-published, 1981.

———. *Packets to Paradise: Steamboating to Paradise*. Missoula, MT: Pictorial Histories Publishing Company, 2001.

Lepley, John G. and Sue, eds. *The Vanishing West: Hornaday's Buffalo: The Last of the Wild Herds*. Big Sandy, MT: Rettig Publishing, n.d.

Morgan, Bob, with Norma Ashby. *Bob Morgan's Montana: My Life and Art*. Helena, MT: Sweetgrass Books of Farcountry Press, 2008.

International Fur Trade Symposium Proceedings 2003: The Fur and Robe Trade in Blackfoot Country, 1831 to 1880. Fort Benton, MT: River and Plains Society, 2003.

Overholser, Joel. *Fort Benton: World's Innermost Port*. Self-published. 1987.

Robison, Ken. *Fort Benton Historian Blog*. www.fortbenton.blogspot.com.

www.nationalregisterofhistoricplaces.com/mt/Chouteau/state.html

INDEX

ABOUT THE RIVER
AND PLAINS SOCIETY

Over the decades, many people and organizations have worked to preserve the history of Fort Benton. History and historical preservation have been the passion of many along the way. Once the first museum, the Museum of the Upper Missouri, opened in 1957, the modern era began. The formation of the Montana Agricultural Museum by the Montana State Legislature in 1989 made clear the need for a formal nonprofit organization. The River and Plains Society began operations in 1992 as the umbrella governing body for the growing museums' complex in Fort Benton.

Under executive director John G. Lepley and a broadly based board of trustees, the River and Plains Society operates the Museum of the Upper Missouri; the Museum of the Northern Great Plains with its Montana Agricultural Museum, Homestead Village, and Hornaday Buffalo Room; the Montana Agricultural Center with its community events center; the Fur Trade Museum in the Trade Store of the reconstructed Old Fort Benton; and the Overholser Historical Research Center in the Schwinden Library and Archives. In addition, the River and Plains Society is in partnership with the City of Fort Benton and the Bureau of Land Management to provide artifacts and interpretation at the Upper Missouri Breaks National Monument Interpretive Center.

The Overholser Historical Research Center is a center for historians, writers, students, and local and family history researchers. The center houses a substantial collection of published and unpublished archival records and images of individuals, families, organizations, businesses, and events. Manuscripts, documents, and photographs in the collection are important to each era in the history of Fort Benton.

Except for occasional grants, the River and Plains Society operates without government funding through a combination of annual memberships, private donations, and volunteer staffing. Recent benefactors have contributed major acquisitions, such as the 1856 John Mix Stanley painting of Alexander Culbertson and an 81-print set of Karl Bodmer lithographs. You can help preserve Fort Benton history, share your photographs and memorabilia, and become a member of the River and Plains Society at Box 262, Fort Benton, MT, 59442.

www.arcadiapublishing.com

Discover books about the town where you grew up, the cities where your friends and families live, the town where your parents met, or even that retirement spot you've been dreaming about. Our Web site provides history lovers with exclusive deals, advanced notification about new titles, e-mail alerts of author events, and much more.

MADE IN THE USA

Arcadia Publishing, the leading local history publisher in the United States, is committed to making history accessible and meaningful through publishing books that celebrate and preserve the heritage of America's people and places. Consistent with our mission to preserve history on a local level, this book was printed in South Carolina on American-made paper and manufactured entirely in the United States.

This book carries the accredited Forest Stewardship Council (FSC) label and is printed on 100 percent FSC-certified paper. Products carrying the FSC label are independently certified to assure consumers that they come from forests that are managed to meet the social, economic, and ecological needs of present and future generations.

FSC
Mixed Sources
Product group from well-managed forests and other controlled sources

Cert no. SW-COC-001530
www.fsc.org
© 1996 Forest Stewardship Council

Find *Your* Place in History.